The First Minnesota Regiment at Gettysburg

The First Minnesota Regiment at Gettysburg

by

William & Robert Haiber

The Info Devel Press

Looking west from whence the rebels attacked, with the Codori house in the middle distance, the second, and lesser known, monument to the First Minnesota Regiment. This one marks the spot where they fought on 3 July during Pickett's charge. It is about a quarter-mile north of the main monument shown on the front cover.

The Info Devels Inc
32 Reilly Road
La Grangeville
New York 12540-6121
Telephone: 845.223.3269
E-mail: IDPress@frontiernet.net

Published in 2003
Second edition.
Printed in the United States of America
10 09 08 07 06 05 04 03 10 9 8 7 6 5 4 3 2 1
First printing
Library of Congress cataloguing-in-publication data
Haiber, William & Robert
The First Minnesota Regiment at Gettysburg
1. History—military
2. The American Civil War, 1861–1865
3. Union Army of the Potomac
4. Battle of Gettysburg, PA
I. Haiber, William Paul & Robert Eugene
II. Title
ISBN: 0–944089–39–9
Copyright number: 2002092757

Body text typeset 11/13 Adobe Garamond Pro font; major headings in ITC Garamond Handtooled
Computer hardware: Apple Macintosh G4 800s and PowerBook G3 400 running OSX 10.2.x; UMAX scanners; Xanté Accel-a-Writer and Epson C80 printers for proofing.
Computer software: Adobe Photoshop 7.0, Adobe Indesign 2.x, Adobe Illustrator 10, MS Word: Mac: X.

Dedication

*To: the 1st Minnesota Regiment of Volunteers**

Nature of Casualty: Death

I die here where I lie here
and it's strange how calm it seems
as a thousand blood-stained men around me
fill the air with screams...
the smoking choking raging pain
and maelstrom that surround
now fade into a dream
for I'm embraced by loving ground.

Yes, war's a game of chance,
so I surrender up with grace
and as the dying sun
pours its sweet honey on my face,
I look to Minnesota,
say to all of you, Farewell—
remember what we did here,
remember why we fell.

–Pvt Hell

At the behest of Gen'l Winfield Hancock, ("Charge those lines!") the 262 men of this one-time thousand-man regiment made a virtual suicide charge against 1,600 'Alabamians' of Wilcox's Brigade in the smoking sunset of July 2 at Gettsyburg.

Only 47 'Minnesotians' were left standing, but they preserved the integrity of the Union line, (as did the 20th Maine, a half-mile to the south at about the same time.)

Said Hancock: "There is no more gallant deed recorded in history."

Said Sergeant Alfred Plummer of Company K: "We had no time to weep."

—Notes by Steve Bartel

* Steve Bartel, the author of this poem, has written an magnificent collection of poems on the American civil war, which we will publish in 2003.

Contents

Washington City

April 14, 1861

Hon. Simon Cameron,

Sec'y War

Sir,

As the Executive of the state of Minnesota, I hereby tender to the Government of the U States, on the part of that state, one thousand men, to be ready for service so soon as the necessary information can be communicated to the people there.

As the Legislature is not in Session, and will not be until specially convened, before January of next year, may I ask whether you would feel justified in saying that the reasonable expenses that may be incurred will be furnished by the General Government, in view of the facts above stated?

I am pleased to say that in all this, I have the advice and support of the Senators from Minnesota, and know that it will be heartily and promptly supported to this action.

Very Respectfully

Your obt. ser.

Alex. Ramsey

Illustrations & maps

Cover photograph: the 'main' First Minnesota Regiment of Volunteers monument

June 1863

Monday	Tuesday	Wednesday	Thursday	Friday	Saturday	Sunday
					Minnesota 1st at Falmouth below Stacy House, recuperating from the second Fredericksburg battle. 1	Couch transferred to Dept of Susquehanna. Hancock to command II Corps. Wm Harrow to lead Sully's Brigade. 2
Col Morgan resigns: bad health. Wm Colvill is new colonel; Chas Adams promoted to Lt Col. Mark Downie upped to major. 3	Sully goes to Minnesota to put down the Indians. He is given a $1,000 sword and a parade. 4	5	Hooker sends VI Corps across Rappahanock at the Franklin crossing; then he goes back to sleep. 6	7	8	1st Minn parades for 34th NY at railhead as 30K two–year men get mustered out. 9
10	11	12	Hooker recalls VI Corps. Lee's ANV in the Shenandoah Valley. Federal horse at Blue Ridge passes. 13	Hooker puts AOP in motion. 1st Minn is rearguard, but after five-mile hike recalled to Falmouth picket duty. 14	First light; march to Stafford CH. At 1400 hrs marches to, and crosses Aquia Creek to camp several miles beyond. 15	0300 resume march. Breakfast 0700 at Dumfries. Bivouac north bank of the Occoquan by 1800. 16
At Sangster's Station, several men drop from heat prostration and sunstroke. 17	18	Regiment moves south to Centreville near the old Bull Run battlefield. 19	Minnesota Reg't pillages 9th Mass sutler's tent. Rolls cannon downhill; marches via battlefield to Gainesville. 20	March north of Gainesville to Thoroughfare Gap to guard passes. Stay to 25 June. 21	Thoroughfare Gap 22	Thoroughfare Gap 23
Thoroughfare Gap 24	In forenoon move to Haymarket to foil Stuart's attack on 2nd Division wagon trains. Arty gets Colvill's horse; wounds 2 men. 25	1200 hrs cross Potomac at Edward's Ferry and bivouac near 1861 camp. 26	27	At the Monocacy overlooking town of Frederick. Meade given command of the Army of the Potomac. 28	31-mile march to Uniontown on the PA line. Picket action. 29	Pay Call: 27 officers; 358 men. Uniontown people hold ball; dancers from reg't dance, as Gettysburg battle opens. 30

Introduction

Birth certificate

THE FIRST MINNESOTA Regiment of Volunteers was born on 14 April 1861, when Alexander Ramsey, governor of Minnesota, on a visit to Washington, wrote a tender of 1,000 troops to Secretary of War, Simon Cameron. The tender was accepted by President Lincoln who issued a call on the 15th for 75,000 volunteers to serve 90 days to suppress the rebellion started at Fort Sumter, on a small island in Charleston harbor, South Carolina. The time: 4.30am, Friday, 12 April. For the Union soldiers at the fort, it was too early for morning guns, but not for the artillerists under the command of General Gustave Tousaint Beauregard.

Maternity ward

Organized at Fort Snelling, in St Paul, Minnesota, the First Regiment of Minnesota Volunteers consisted of ten infantry companies: A, B, C, D, E, F, G, H, I, K. Each company of one hundred men was recruited from the state militia companies and the male population of military age. By 29 April, ten companies had assembled at Fort Snelling. The Stars and Stripes was run up the halyard, a 34-gun salute was fired, and an al fresco dinner was served to the men and their guests.

Baptisms and anointments

That afternoon the men were inspected and Captain Nelson of the Regular Army swore the men into Federal service. Governor Alexander Ramsey appointed Willis Gorman, colonel; Stephen Miller, lieutenant colonel; and William Dike, major. Colonel Gorman then appointed Lieutenant Thomas Foster regimental quartermaster. Dr. Jacob Stewart was appointed regimental surgeon. Next day Charles Le Boutiller was appointed assistant surgeon and Lieutenant William Leach was appointed adjutant.

The guns of April

Various shoulder weapons, were carried by the troops: Militia companies reported Springfield rifles. Some reported with Mississippi rifles and sword bayonets. Still others bore weapons from the state arsenal. The Springfields were retained, and a .69 caliber musket, said to be effective, was substituted for the others.

The State of Minnesota furnished each man with a blanket, a flannel shirt, and a pair of socks. On 9 May, they were issued black felt hats, black trousers, and red flannel shirts. Exceptions were the men of Company K (Captain Lester) who wore the grey uniforms given them by the citizens of Winona.

Upping the ante

On 10 May, on the suggestion of the Secretary of War, Captain Nelson remustered the troops for three year's service. Men declining this were mustered out and their places filled by new enlistments. By 24 May, the Regiment was at full strength.

Boat rides and footraces

On 28 May, Major Dike with Company B and Captain McKune with G Company steamed upriver on the "Frank Steel" to relieve two companies of the First Infantry (US) at Fort Ridgely on the Minnesota River.

On 29 May, Captain Wilkin marched A Company to Fort Ripley to relieve two companies of the Second Infantry (US) for further duty at the seat of the war.

On 6 June, Captain Morgan marched E Company to Fort Ripley and met Abercrombie's companies on their way back to Fort Snelling.

On 10 June, Lt Col Miller took C Company (Capt Acker) and D Company (Capt Putnam) on a march to Fort Abercrombie, but as these companies had to go over one hundred miles to the fort, they were in transit when the word came to Ramsey on 14 June that the Regiment was to report to Washington DC via Harrisburg, Pennsylvania. Gorman then sent messengers to recall the detached companies.

By 21 June all of the companies, but Wilkin's A Company and 25 men of G Company, had returned to Fort Snelling. Morgan's E Company, fearing that Gorman would leave on Friday, marched all night on Thursday to reach the fort by Friday morning.

Au revoir, Minnesota

At 5am, 22 June, the Regiment was broken out; religious services were conducted by Edward D Neil, regimental chaplain; and the whole kit and caboodle was boarded on two steamers, "War Eagle" and "Northern Belle": the first went to Prairie du Chien; the second to Lacrosse, both in Wisconsin, from which places first-class coaches carried the troops via Janesville to arrive at Chicago at 6pm, 23 June.

Chicago, that wonderful town

Chicago mayor John Wentworth complimented the boys, and marched with them from the Northwest Depot to the Pittsburgh and Fort Wayne Depot through crowded streets.

The Chicago Tribune reported: *"There are few regiments we have ever seen that can compare in brawn and muscle with these Minnesotans, used to the axe, the rifle, the oar and the setting pole. They are unquestionably the finest body of troops that has yet appeared in our streets."*

The Regiment arrived in Harrisburg, PA at 10pm on 25 June, entering a nearby camp of instruction. At 3am on 26 June, they rode cattle cars to Baltimore, a city noted for its southern sympathizers. Consequently, the march to the Washington depot was made with fixed bayonets and charged weapons, but the cars were boarded without incident: They reached Washington about 10pm.

First coffee break

The Minnesota regiment was welcomed to the Capitol by Colonel Cyrus Aldrich, ex-Minnesota congressman. His staff provided coffee, sandwiches, and other refreshments, in the Assembly rooms where the regiment spent the night: there and in the Congregational Church.

The 1st Regiment spent several days drilling at Camp Minnesota near the unfinished Capitol building. On 28 June, Wilkin's A Company, wearing the uniforms they secured at Fort Ripley, reported for duty. On 3 July, the regiment took steamers from the Navy Yard to Alexandria, Virginia. There they went into Camp Franklin and bivouacked along the Alexandria–Fairfax Road.

In the Army now

The 1st Regiment was soon attached, with the 5th and 11th Massachusetts regiments and Battery I, First US Artillery, to the First Brigade (Gen William B Franklin) of the Third Division (Gen Samuel P Heintzelman) of the Army of Northern Virginia (Irvin McDowell, general commanding). When the Army of the Potomac was organized under McClellan this designation disappeared from Union nomenclature, but was assumed by Robert E Lee, when he took command of Confederate forces after the "Seven Days" battles before Richmond.

The 1st Regiment spent most of July guarding the telegraph line along the Orange and Alexandria Railroad, by alternating companies of pickets; Companies E, F, and K patrolled as far as Bailey's crossroads without coming across an enemy soldier.

First report card

On 11 July, Colonel Gorman reported to Governor-Ramsey that the Minnesota 1st "was the best drilled, best disciplined Regt. in the service and such is the judgt of the Regular officers that have seen us".

On 13 July, Captain McKune's Fort Abercrombie detachment reported to Colonel Gorman. The First was at full strength.

On 15 July, the men drew three day's rations against marching orders: all equipment, except necessary field equipment, was turned in to the quartermaster at Alexandria.

Some bulls walked

On the 16th, the First Minnesota (minus one hundred on the sick-list and camp guards) marched 12 miles toward Manassas Junction. They camped on the high ground near Powick Creek. From there, on the 17th, they marched 16 miles to Sangster's Station on the Orange and Alexandria O and A) Railroad. The march was delayed by enemy rearguards who felled trees to create roadblocks to delay the Union army. On the 18th, the Regiment made bivouac at Centreville off the Warrenton Pike. At Bull Run, the ten companies of the 1st Minnesota would enter the first of the several engagements that would, by the time of Gettysburg, virtually destroy the regiment as an organization that still contained human beings.

Some considerations

Minnesota, at the time the Civil War began, was still a frontier State, having been admitted into the Union in 1859. Most of the settlers were directed to Minnesota by American recruiters who offered land to any European who would settle on the frontier lands of America, which was then called the "Land of opportunity". The Germans, Scandanavians, and other Nordic races who came to Minnesota moved to a land that was not too much different from what they knew in their mother countries. It was different, however, in that it was a largely unsettled and they had to share it with Sioux and Ojibway tribes who strongly resisted encroachment on their sacred hunting grounds. Many of the settlers, with the administrative and technical skills of civilization, came from eastern States: lawyers, engineers, mechanics, doctors, clergymen, lawmen, and politicians. It is a matter of record that, of the whole 1st Minnesota roster, only eight men had been born in Minnesota. In the country at large, the majority of troops in the Union army were German and Irish immigrants who accepted the recruiters challenge and became Americans the hard way—by working for it on their own land, under a government 'by the people' and not of kings. When they said that America was a 'melting pot' they meant that when the 'melting' was finally completed, the cultural soup that would be poured into the bowls of society would be American. Outside of the culinary diversity of the American menu and the diversity of family names, American cultural forms have voluntarily been accepted by the common people of Europe; the chiefest of which are found in the Bill of Rights, one of the founding document of this nation: cultural forms by which Europeans have banished totalitarian governments imposed without the consent of the people.

That is why, when it came to preserving the Union as 'one Nation, indivisible' the young men of Minnesota got themselves to Fort Snelling. One recruit named Charles Brown walked 50 miles barefoot to signup. The Italians have a proverb: "Between saying and doing is the depth of the sea", and there is the Biblical expression: "Be not only a sayer of the Word, but a doer of the Word". The first generation of Minnesotans were doers: they built a territory and they converted it into a State; the second generation, equally tough, mostly farm boys and woodsmen supplied eight infantry regiments to the Union army. The Minnesota First, according to a Gettysburg sign, was known as the 'regiment with a reputation' which they had earned by their steadfastness and natural courage in all their battles: Bull Run, Balls Bluff, Seven Pines, the Seven Days, Second Bull Run, Antietam, Fredericksburg, and Chancellorsville, leading up to the climactic battle at Gettysburg. On the 2nd day of July 1863, the First lost about 191 casualties, and on the 3rd of July there were 25 casualties. Total casualties were 216 out of 416 present and available for duty on 30 June: The regiment with a reputation.

Chapter One

Bulls Running

No rest for Judith Henry

ON 21 JULY, a hot Virginia Sunday, the First Minnesota, as part of Sam Heintzelman's Third Division, marched to Bull Run, left the Warrenton Pike in a hooking movement against the left flank of the Confederate Army led by General Pierre Gustave Tousaint Beauregard. The Confederate line lay generally behind Bull Run (a run being more than a brook and less than a creek). The Union attack against the Confederate left, anchored on Bull Run near Sudley Springs, forced the Confederates to retire: first to Matthews Hill, then to Buck Hill; then to the Henry House Hill where they regrouped on General Thomas Jackson's right. The rebel right flank rested on the Robinson House. To thicken this line more regiments came to their aid from the rail depot at Manassas Junction, six miles from their front on the high ground of the Henry House Hill.

The Henry House Hill formed a semicircular plateau. The distance between the Confederate left, at the Henry House, and the Confederate right at the Robinson House was about half a mile. It was on this hill that the right flank of the Union Army clashed with the Confederate left. It was there that Thomas Jackson was nicknamed 'Stonewall' and the men of the Minnesota First learned that earning a reputation was not an easy task.

Let no guns split asunder

In the open ground between the Henry House and the Sudley-Manassas Road, the ten guns of Rickett's and Griffith's Batteries were unlimbered, after passing through Companies A and F of the Minnesota First after they had crossed Young's Branch. Companies A and F formed on the right of, and the other eight companies, along with the 11th New York formed on the left of the batteries.

Captain, later Colonel, Colvill described the Regiment's movements: *"We filed left, in to a field, and then up the hill, coming by company into line, and then forward into line, with the intent to form on the brink of the hill, the batteries to pass through the line at the centre, taking positions a short distance in front."*

Early was not late enough

The action in and around these Griffith's and Rickett's Batteries lasted about two hours (4 to 6pm). The situation they found themselves in was confused. Sam Stebbins wrote: *"One of the cannons stood directly behind me, and I heard the officer of the gun order his man to shoot us down if we did not get out of the way; and as I saw him about to execute the order, I stepped forward out of the ranks and to the right, when the gun went off, and nearly knocked me down."*

Stebbins, firing at the rebels, was wounded when a soldier standing near him was mortally wounded from a shot. As he toppled forward, the bayonette on his musket pierced the instep of Stebbins's right foot. Pinned to the ground, it took a minute or two for Stebbins to free himself.

During the fighting, the wounded Stebbins became separated from the Regiment. Casting about for some protection, he found none.

"At this time, the artillerymen had left the cannon, and every horse was dead, and the Minnesota Regiment had moved to the right and left of me.

"I loaded and fired several times while standing there. There were several of the Minnesota Regiment lying dead in front of me, but they all lay on their faces, so I could not tell who they were, and the fire was too hot for me to stop and examine them. At last, an officer of the Zouaves ordered us to retreat and take to the woods, but as I ran

down the hill, I saw the blood running out of my shoe. I sat down to examine my foot, and when I got my shoe on again, I saw our boys coming back, and the rebels had possession of the cannon that had been left by our artillery, and were turning them against us. As I was lame, I thought it best for me to take care of myself, and, accorodingly, started with a man that had a shot through his arm, for the hospital, but he could travel faster than I, and left me as I was passing off from the field."

The guns were captured and recaptured in a see-saw struggle terminated by Early's attack on the Union right. The shock of this attack caused an instant withdrawal, that turned into a partial rout for the Blues, and signalled victory for General P T G Beauregard and his men.

Captain Colvill described his experiences during the withdrawal:

"As I was about to start from the scene of the last action, near the guns, I heard a man crying, and saw a soldier sitting on the ground, and went to him. He had dragged himself from the wood, and was crying at seeing us leave, thinking himself abandoned. His leg was broken, the bone prutruding. I quieted him, and, seeing a troop of our cavalry, hurried back. Just then, one of the cavalry exclaimed, 'The devils are coming,' and every horse whisked about, and the cavalry was off like a streak. I turned to see what was the matter, as a platoon of the enemy was making a wheeel out of the woods to the right in to the road. Their sweep would have taken me in. Instinctively, I broke for the ravine. As I reached it, I heard the chuck of the muskets, as they fell forward in to the left hands, and dropped on my back on the slope, as the bullets buzzed like a nest of hornets past my head. I sprang up and, glancing back, saw a row of blank faces, astonished at seeing me break down the ravine, soon out of their fire. When I reached the brook, three or four of our men were drinking. A Wisconsin man dropped dead in the brook as we started. A Fire Zouave jumped the brook at my side, and ran up the hill. He also dropped, but with my help, reached the top and the shelter of a tree."

The music faced or the elephant seen

The term "partial rout" is used because not all Federal or volunteer units granulated when fear overcame discipline.

The two right companies of the 1st Minnesota retreated by way of the Sudley Road, joining the companies of the left that had retreated to Buck Hill. Fom there the Regiment moved back to their Centreville bivouac, then to Camp Minnesota on the Capitol grounds.

In this fight, the Minnesotans fought with Jackson's men at the batteries and drove them from the guns on two occasions.

They suffered more casualties than any regiment engaged: Casualties were estimated at 34 killed, 120 wounded, four wounded prisoners; five healthy prisoners (includes two surgeons) = 163. Others say 184, 185, or 190 casualties. The above casualties are taken from the company rosters listed in "Minnesota in the Civil and Indian Wars", compiled in 1890. The Regiment reported 1,023 officers and men on 26 June. Subtract the 100 sick men left in camp, 923 men could have done some fighting. First Minnesota casualties equalled 17.6% of those engaged.

One plus was that they captured Colonel Boone of the 4th Georgia, the highest-ranking officer captured on either side. Another plus was Sergeant John G Merritt of K Company who was awarded the Congressional Medal of Honor for his actions that day.

After the battle, Sergeant Joseph Spencer wrote: *"I know what it is to stand where musket balls are thick as hail, and to have cannon balls, grape shot, and bomb shell falling in every direction. I know what it is to have our lines broken and our men scattered, and to have them rally again around the good old Stars and Stripes. I know what it is to have our forces defeated, but thank God not a cowardly or shameful defeat."*

Chapter Two

Ball's Bluff—Not Ours

Changes of address

After Bull Run, there were changes in the Regiment. Colonel Gorman, was promoted to brigadier, and replaced by Napoleon Dana, West Pointer and veteran of the Mexican War. Major Dike resigned, and was replaced by Captain George Morgan. Major Wilkin transferred, as colonel, to the 9th Minnesota. Lieutenant Coates moved to H Company as a captain. Several enlisted men moved up as officers. Recruiters were sent to Minnesota to bring the regiment to full strength; by mid-August they had sent 120 replacements to the First Regiment at Camp Stone, Named for General Stone, the camp was located two miles from the Potomac river between Edwards Ferry and Poolesville. By the time it participated in the action at Ball's Bluff on 21 October, the Regiment was altogether a different animal. It was blooded and looking for blood.

Asking for it

The Union Army contained two armies: the very small Regular Army of trained professionals; and an army of volunteer regiments. The volunteer regiments were organized at the state level under the control of the governor via the state adjutant general who communicated with Simon F Cameron, secretary of war, (later replaced by Edwin M Stanton, 13 January 1862). Commissions were issued at the state level on a mostly political basis and seconded by the War Department; it was this political dealing in commissions that gave command to too many men who had no military experience. This military patronage existed at the Federal level too, so that when the various regiments were formed into brigades, the brigades into divisions, the divisions into army corps, and the army corps into armies, battles would be won by the side with the fewest incompetent officers in the command structure. It all looked good on paper as all paper armies usually do. The enlisted men could not buy their stripes and they generally fought well, even under bad leaders. They proved it over and over again despite their numerous losses. The situation changed when officer review boards were set up to purge the Army of its incompetents, where possible. Politics being what it always was, the upper echelons were mainly exempt.

The action at Ball's Bluff, also called the Battle of Leesburg, was an example of what happens when sincere men think that bravery alone is a sufficient substitute for military expertise. In an army where the blind were leading those who could see, mistakes meant falling bodies and oozing blood.

George McClellan replaced McDowell after Bull Run, and the Army of Northern Virginia was renamed the Army of the Potomac. McClellan's first offensive action was to order General Charles P Stone's Division to probe the Confederate forces opposite him at Leesburg. Stone's orders were to determine if the Confederate forces under General Evans, were going to move on Manassas. Stone's plan of action was to march his division to Edward's Ferry, where he ordered Colonel Napoleon Dana (the new commander of the 1st Minnesota) to embark the St. Anthony and Winona companies in two boats, cross the Potomac, and send out patrols. After landing, the Minnesotans dispersed enemy pickets: a Mississippi infantry company and a cavalry detachment. The Minnesota infantry then recrossed to the Maryland side of the Potomac to await further orders.

Autumn leaves

On the morning of 21 October, General Stone pushed 2,000 men, mostly from Gorman's Brigade, to divert rebel attention from the Union force that was crossing the Potomac to Ball's Bluff via Harrison's Island, four miles upriver from Edward's Ferry. Operating out of Fort Evans at Leesburg, the Confederate force was commanded by Brigadier General Nathan Evans. This was the same Evans who, at Bull Run, made what many consider the finest tactical maneuver of the battle: Evans held the right flank of the rebel line at the stone bridge but, seeing Union forces approaching his left rear, he left a small covering force, and marched the main body to successfully block General Burnside's brigade, and blunt the Union advance, prior to Early's attack.

At Ball's Bluff, Evans developed his force of 2,000 men with such skill that he surrounded the Union force on the bluff, fought it off and pushed Stone's soldiers off the 70-foot height.

The loss to the Federals: 49 killed, 198 wounded, more than a 100 drowned and 259 captured. Casualties came to more than 35.6% of the 1,700 engaged. Evans's men lost: 36 killed, 117 wounded, and two missing. It was said of Evans that he fought this battle dead drunk. For the First Minnesota, it meant one man killed and two wounded, at Edward's Ferry while on patrol, on 23 October.

Stone goes to the hard place

Ball's Bluff demonstrated how difficult it is for brave, but militarily ignorant men to win battles. Colonel Baker, who had taken command of the regiments on the bluff, broke enough tactical rules to cost him a bullet between the eyes. But, being a close friend of Lincoln, his blunders were overlooked. Instead, it was General Stone, who had done nothing wrong, who was thrown into the brig at Governor's Island, in New York harbor. He was vilified in the press on rumors of sedition. It is one thing to tell a man what to do, but quite another to get him to remember to do it when the time comes. The irony of it all was that Nathan Evans, the rebel commander, was the same Evans who had blunted the Union flank attack against the rebel left at Bull Run, a man whose tactical skills were not blunted by the whiskey he drank.

The Minnesota First returned to Camp Stone, to resume picket duties along the Potomac and continue drill schedules in company, regimental and brigade maneuvering. On 16 January, Brigadier John Sedgwick assumed command of the division, relieving General Stone. February 3rd saw the promotion of Colonel Dana to brigadier in that division. On 13 March, Colonel Alfred Sully took command of the 1st Minnesota as it left camp at Berryville, Virginia. Colonel Sully, a West Pointer, who had fought in the Mexican and Seminole Wars, was the senior captain in the Regular Army. His father, Alfred Sully, was the noted American portraitist.

Sully marched the Regiment toward Winchester, in pursuit of Stonewall Jackson, who faded in retreat. The 1st Regiment returned its blistered feet to the Berryville bivouac.

Little Mac's baby

On 15 March, Sully's troops were camped on Bolivar Heights above Harpers Ferry. It was there that the organization of the Army of the Potomac into corps was announced. The Minnesota First was placed in Napoleon Dana's Brigade of John Sedgwick's 2nd Division of Edwin Sumner's II Corps. By the night of 26 March, the Regiment was back at the old Bull Run camp. There the sodden troops dug up a barrel of whiskey (stolen from their sutler) to toast their participation in the Valley Campaign, and insulate themselves against the torrential rain that fell on them. There was more marching and fighting ahead: in the ill fated Peninsular Campaign, at Antietam, at Fredericksburg, and at Chancellorsville. Georges Clemenceau observed that "War was too important an affair to be left in the hands of the generals". That observation certainly applied, in the beginning, to the generalship in the Civil War, because there were no competent generals to be had. The only general who knew how to conduct that war was Winfield Scott, a veteran of the Revolutionary War, and the commander who saw the Stars and Stripes raised over Santa Anna's Mexico. When Scott retired, General George McClellan took his place, but it was Scott's 'Anaconda' plan that won the war when it was executed by General U S Grant.

Chapter Three

The Peninsular Campaign

The Peninsular Campaign may be described in two parts: the first was the battle of Fair Oaks or Seven Pines; the second was the Seven Days battle fought by the Army of Northern Virginia, under General Robert E Lee who replaced General Joseph E Johnson when the latter was wounded seriously in the arm and chest.

In these battles, we see the First Minnesota, hardened by more than ten month's drilling, marching, picketing and battle experience, showing its true grit at crucial points: it contributed to the Union victory at Seven Pines and it kept the retreat, via the 'grapevine bridge' which the Minnesotans built, to Harrison's Landing from being a complete rout.

Seven Pines beats Fair Oaks

On 4 May 1862, the siege of Yorktown ended with the evacuation of the Confederate works, and the Minnesota First left its soggy billets at Camp Misery to pursue a soggy enemy.

Under heavy fire from enemy batteries, on 8 May, the troops disembarked from the Long Branch at West Point, on the Upper York River. From there they went by boat to Eltham's Landing to camp for seven days when they performed picket duties along the Richmond and York Railroad.

By 23 May, the Regiment, in division, camped near the Tyler House on the north side of the Chickahominy River which diagonally divided the 800 square mile battlefield.

On the 27 May, the Regiment marched to the swollen river and built the Grapevine Bridge, so called because wild grapevines were used to hold the bridge together.

On the 31st, the Regiment crossed this bridge, almost afloat in the rain-swollen river, to support Couch's right flank in Courtney's wheatfield. From behind a rail fence they overlapped the rebel left flank (the 4th Alabama, 2nd Mississippi and Law's Brigade) into which they poured an effective crossfire. They gave a lot of fire and took very little. Casualties were two killed and four wounded.

The other units of their brigade, in action for the first time, the 82nd and the 34th NY, on Couch's left, led a bayonet charge spurred on by General Sumner's order, "Charge 'em with the bayonet, General Gorman!". They saved Rickett's Battery, and forced the enemy left to give way. A large number of prisoners were taken including a colonel, a lieutenant colonel, and two company officers of the 6th North Carolina Regiment. The rebel colonel, by coincidence, had been a lieutenant in Sully's company in the Regular Army. This operation cost the Regiment two killed, and one wounded. Another died by friendly fire on the picket line. The wounding of General Johnston worked against the Union army: It brought Lee to command for the Seven Days which ended McClellan's attempt to capture Richmond and end the war.

Seven Days with the wrong general

After Seven Pines, it was McClellan's intention to besiege Richmond rather than carry it by direct assault. To do this meant bringing up heavy artillery on roads that would have to dry out enough to support their weight. General Lee, now commander of the Army of Northern Virginia, knew that if McClellan got his guns up, he could blast his way into Richmond. While 'Little Mac' took his time, Lee sent his army to attack Fitz John Porter's isolated corps north of the Chicahominy at Mechanicsville. To do this he brought Jackson out of the Shenandoah Valley and other reserves from Charleston to form an attack force of 57,000 troops. Lee opened the battle on 26 June, with attacks on Porter by the divisions of generals Longstreet, A P Hill, and D H Hill. They attacked again and again, but were repulsed each time, with heavy losses.

At this point, McClellan lost his nerve and ordered an unnecessary retreat.

From Mechanicsville, the Army of the Potomac was pushed south for seven days: to Gaines' Mill (Cold Harbor), across the Chicahominy by New Bridge; Allen's Farm (part of the Fair Oaks battlefield); Savage Station where the First Minnesota tangled with Kershaw's troops. The 1st Minnesota suffered four killed and 44 wounded, most of whom had to be left for enemy medics. The retreat continued across White Oak Swamp. At Glendale, the bill was one killed and five wounded. Back down the Peninsula they went, nudged by the rebels. The retreat ended on 1 July at Malvern Hill where Union artillery and Berdan's Sharpshooters brought Lee's counter-offensive to a halt. The week's losses: 20,000 Confederate to 15,849 Union's.

The tragedy of it all, for the Union, was that, at the time McClellan decided to retreat, the rebels were greatly demoralized by their defeat at Fair Oaks/ Seven Pines: the citizens of Richmond were fleeing and the Confederate government was moving its public records to safety. Shaken troops held the outer line of the city's defences, and Lee assumed that McClellan would resume his offensive. Fitz John Porter, who had broken the rebel left, urged McClellan to let him attack the rebel flank via Mechanicsville, but the ever cautious McClellan rejected Fitz John's scheme.

Even after Gaines' Mill, where the Confederates lost 7,800 to the Union's 4,000, Lee thought George McClellan would attack and prevail.

The night of the battle, a council of officers was convened. To quote Dr Dabney, from his book on Jackson:

"After many painful details of losses and disasters, they all concurred in declaring that McClellan would probably take the aggressive in the morning and that the Confederate army could not resist him."

They needn't have worried. From this point on Lee, who had served with McClellan in the Mexican War, was confident that he could defeat McClellan any time he met him, but he also realized that he would have to decisively beat the Union army and that would take a lot more doing than spooking McClellan's mind. Lee issued his attack orders and gambled the fate of the Confederacy on the bravery and endurance of his shaken army.

Viewed statistically, the Peninsular campaign was a Union victory. Viewed strategically, McClellan's campaign was a failure, not because of anything Lee did, but a failure because of what McClellan failed to do, namely to keep attacking with the resources at his command. Although he was called "The Boy Napoleon" there was nothing Napoleonic about his style of command. Where as Napoleon was up front with his troops, McClellan stayed behind the front at his headquarters blinded by a fog of war that existed only in his own mind. He reminds one of the person who insists on waiting for a weather report to confirm the downpour he can observe from his own window.

When McClellan ordered the Union retreat, Lee could have got the Union army back into the boats at Harrison's landing by not pushing so hard, yet he put his men through the grinder. His last attack at Malvern hill cost five thousand men. A Union counter-attack could have saved McClellan's bacon.

Looking toward the future, the Union army made up not only its losses, but steadily increased the size of its armies, and its logistics base. While Lee, drawing replacements from a southern population of sixteen million and an even smaller military population, could never make all of his losses good. The naval blockade and the Union drive up and down the Mississippi by the Western army was realizing Scott's Anaconda plan of slowly squeezing the Confederacy in on itself. Lee's men were always on short rations and wanting for shoes. Lee was learning that bravery without beans eventually means a lost war.

Chapter Four

The Bulls Run Again

Another Bad General

After the Seven Days battles, Halleck was appointed general-in-chief of the Union armies: Halleck was an old line regular, known for his attention to detail and was nicknamed 'Old Brains'. He could generate a brilliant plan for campaign, but by the time it took him to transmit those plans to the assault forces, the military situation changed to invalidate the plan. He was an honest and sincere soldier but he could not determine the transition point from theory to practice. His only real test at command came when he assumed command of Grant's arm after Shiloh. The rebels were in retreat. It took Halleck something like thirty days to move Grant's army to Corinth. Halleck had his soldiers dig in every night. On approaching Corinth, he encircled the town with rings of entrenchments. While Halleck's men were doing this, the rebels ran boxcars up to this railhead, evacuating a rebel army he could have had for the taking, using a little 'celerity' as they said in those times.

It should be taken into consideration that the Civil War was an ad hoc operation from the beginning for both sides. In a country which had no use for standing armies and the large infrastructure, either before or after a war, it is amazing how both sides expanded into their logistics lines to accommodate the attrition of war.

If we focus on the Eastern Theater of Operations, it appears that the Confederates were having all of the success: Bull Run, Ball's Bluff, The Peninsular Campaign, Gaines Mill, Seven Pines, and Fair Oaks, but they were paying more in casualties for their success than the Unionists were for their failures, but out of an army almost twice the size of Lee's.

On the Western front, the Union was having all of the success militarily, using the Mississippi, the Tennessee, and Cumberland rivers to guarantee logistic schedules using riverboats rather than hard to protect rails in open country occupied by rebel raiders. Tennessee, Missouri and Kentucky were secured, and the 'Ole Miss' was Union down to Shiloh. The only holdout on the river, Vicksburg, a year away from Grant's army: "Send me men 10 feet tall to dig in mud eight feet deep."

Wars are conducted by means of strategy, tactics, and logistics. Strategy is the master plan by which one side proposes to use its military and civilian resources (men and materiel) to force from its adversary what it could not obtain by the dulcet tones of diplomacy. Tactics are the actual means by which the requirements of strategy are performed. The term 'operational art' is used to describe how tactical commanders conduct military operation in conformance with strategic directives. Logistics, formerly the bugaboo of soldiers and historians, is the third and absolutely necessary element, without which no war is possible. Dr James Huston wrote a beautiful and elegant book on logistics: "The Sinews of War: Army Logistics 1775-1953", Center of Military History, Washington, D C. Read this book and it is possible to track the successes and failures of armies as functions of logistics operations. Colonel Huston was an operations officer for an infantry battalion: 134 Infantry in the ETO WWII). What he wrote about logistics relied more on experience than on theory. He wrote: *"Strategy and tactics and logistics are different aspects of the same thing."* These aspects are completely equivalent. He stated, *"It is difficult to find instances in modern war where a decidedly stronger economic power ultimately has succumbed to a weaker."*

In the coming battle, another professional Union general (Pope) gets whipped tactically by professional Confederates (Lee, Jackson) at Bull Run again by completely committing a logistically inferior army to the demolition of a logistically superior army.

He created a new Army of Virginia with General

John Pope as its commander. It was this army that Lee tore apart and defeated at Second Bull Run, in August 1862.

Again, it was the old reliable First Minnesota, as part of the rear guard, that held the rebels off long enough for Pope to find refuge behind Washington's fortifications and guns.

During the night of 2 September, the First Minnesota and two guns from Battery A, Rhode Island Artillery, stopped the rebel pursuit, disengaged to march north to Vienna, VA, where they were accidentally shot up (now called 'friendly fire') by NY cavalry such that two men were killed and seven were wounded. By 4 September, the troops were in Tennallyton, having shut the door on another Union disaster.

This trouncing of John Pope made Lee believe he could invade the North, and that nothing could stop him. Lee's belief was based on his tactical successes against Union armies led by generals incompetent or unwilling to command and control large units. In the pre-war Regular Army of about 18,000 men, scattered in detachments of company or troop size units, who among the officer corps had hands-on experience beyond company size units? Battalion? Brigade? Division? Corps? Who among all of the officers had ever fought against an enemy in command of large units? And this applies to the Confederacy, whose officer corps was created out of several hundred men who had resigned their Regular Army commissions, to accept higher Confederate army rank. We see Beauregard, a captain at Fort Sumter, receiving salutes as a general at Bull Run after but 90 days in grey. Lee had the opportunity to keep West Virginia in the Union at the very beginning of the war, but let the chance go by. Strategically, West Virginia was the true unopposed gateway into the North, but Lee's first failure turned this new state into a plug that secured the geographical Union right.

With Lee's men on half-rations, did he believe he could beat the Federal army logistically by invading the North?

The logistics or supply function is summed up neatly by Bedford Forrest's homily: "Get thar fustest with the mostest." Defined militarily:

Thar: There = the required place of battle.

Fustest: Be at the place of battle first (before the enemy).

Mostest: Have more troops at the place of battle; have more ammunition; have more rations; have more reinforcements; and have more will-to-win.

Forrest was a cavalry raider who rarely failed in any of his operations which were directed against the logistics system of the Union army—which is to say against the material the enemy was moving toward the battle area. But so vast was the Union logistics system it could tolerate these raids and still meet the demands of an expanding army. And the main function of any commander is that he was responsible for providing his armies with the means of battle: beans and bullets.

An example of logistics inferiority was Hannibal's invasion of Roman Italy. Using double envelopment tactics, he was able to defeat three large Roman armies, but he could not take Rome because he had no siege equipment and not enough of an army to encircle the walls of Rome. He spent 16 frustrating years chasing Fabian the Delayer up and down the peninsular and got nothing for his pains. It took Scipio Africanus one year to defeat Hannibal on his own territory at Zama in 202BC, In one hot afternoon, Africanus eliminated Carthage as a Mediterranean power and established a peace that was to last over 50 years.

Briefly stated logistics superiority is a function of population, and what that population can supply in the way of soldiers and war materiel needed to exercise the strategy and tactics by which wars are won. In the case of Hannibal, he was never logistically superior to the Romans in men and materiel; while he was marching his army to death, the Romans were taking Spain away from Carthage. And building alliances in Africa that would eventually deprive Hannibal of maneuver room in 202.

At Antietam, the logistically superior Union army threw away a decisive victory when McClellan refused to use all of his logistic power.

Chapter Five

Antietam: the Little Mac Attack

Bumbling Blunders

POPE'S FAILURE BROUGHT McClellan back to command. Such was his popularity that the morale of the defeated army rose to new heights. They put Second Bull Run behind them, as they had so many other defeats. By 5 September, the Army of the Potomac was on its feet again and ready for another brawl.

But first, it had to catch the Army of Northern Virginia, which had started its first 'northern invasion.

Ed Walker describes what he saw as he manched north into Maryland with the First Minnesota.

"The next day we kept on, Sesech retreating till we came in sight of South Mountain, could see the smoke of our artillery, and that of the Rebs contesting the pass through the mountains. Saturday in the afternoon we made a short halt, barely time to eat, when we were hurried on towards the firing as night came on, we could see flashes of musketry and artillery, but the distance was so great we could not hear any report. We knew there must be quite a fight going on.... On we marched, dark as pitch, over all sorts of places, till late at night we reached the field, met ambulances and stretchers carrying off the wounded..... Our brigade was put to the front on picket, and we expected to begin the fight in the morning. Our men had had a hard fight, but had drove them, and we held the field.

Private Charles Berry also remembered that night.

"We camped there all night with the dead and dying all around us. The next morning, I looked over the ground to our front, and it was covered with the dead bodies of our enemies. There I saw a rebel sitting on a rock with a woman's picture in his hand, as though he were looking at it, but he was dead.

On 17 September, it would fight the bloodiest battle of the war, a battle which cost both armies about 26,000 killed, wounded and missing. Called the Battle of Antietam, by the North and Sharpsburg by the South, this battle was a strategic, if not a tactical, defeat for General Lee in that it ended his invasion of the North; did not get him any Maryland recruits; did not get the Confederate States foreign recognition; left him with half the troops he had gone north with; and did not keep the Yankees away from the fertile Virginia farmlands. Antietam also showed Lee that the Army of the Potomac was not a quitting army—it only had a quitting general. It wanted to win at Antietam, and would have, but for the refusal of its commander to use his 25,000-man reserve.

In this battle, the Minnesota First was part of Sumner's flawed attack. They fought in the Cornfield, in the West Woods, and around the Dunker Church, but a gap between Richardson's left and Gorman's right opened: Jackson's men charged in to strip the supports from the Minnesotans, who held the right flank of the brigade, forcing all to retreat to the north.

A few weeks after the battle, Sergeant Walker recalled the fighting in the Cornfield.

"We advanced over the ground gained by Hooker, he had just been taken off the field wounded, and his men were exhausted. As we moved on, the dead and wounded lay thick, and fragments of regiments cheered us as we passed. Our men and Secesh lay as they fell, many begging us for a drink of water, others telling us not to tread on them, and it was difficult to march over the ground without stepping on some man.'

After crossing the Cornfield, the Regiment passed through the West Woods and came upon massed rebel infantry and artillery. Colonel Gorman wrote: *"The enemy's heavy lines of infantry first came in to view, the front of which retired in considerable disorder before our advance. We pursued them until we passed the strip of woods and emerged in to the edge of a field.... Instantly, my whole brigade became hotly engaged, giving and receiving the most deadly fire it has ever been my lot to witness. Although the firing was not so rapid, it was most deadly, and at very close range. we also had to stand the most terrific fire of grape and canister, which told fearfully on the three right regiments of the brigade."*

Edward Walker describes what he saw from the edge of the wood.

"Our regiment was close to a rail fence and a corn field between us and the enemy's battery. This battery was on a hill about 700 yards to our right—directly in front of us was their infantry, about 300 yards distant, at the commencement of the fight. As soon as we got into the proper position, both sides commenced peppering one another. Our company fired a few shots at the artillerymen, but as the distance was so great , we directed most of our shots at the rebel colors. They came down several times, but the men stuck to them well. A piece of the staff found after the fight had several ball marks on it, and had been cut away two or three times. We kept firing at what we considered the best marks, every man firing at will, we could see their wounded hobbling to the rear, and some that wasn't wounded, but they seemed to have plenty of re-enforcements.'

The rebel general Lafayette McLaw's found a gap in the Union line and quickly attacked through it. The Union line started to crumble.

Gorman, ever steady, explained what happened next. *"The attack of the enemy on the flank was so sudden, and in such overwhelming force, that I had no time to lose for my command could have been completely enveloped, and probably captured, as the enemy was movingh not only upon my left flank, but also forcing a column toward my right, the two rear lines having both moved from their position before either of my three right regiments changed theirs. Perceiving this, after moving a short distance, my command faced about again toward the enemy and gave him another fire, which to some extent checked his advance. After moving a short distance farther, his forces perceived moving to our right, when the First Minnesota faced toward him and delivered another fire, which again checked his movement."*

Sully reported the Regiment lost 15 killed, 79 wounded and 24 missing—118 casualties out of 435 men, or about 26% of the force engaged, a rate worse than Bull Run.

On 22 September, the First Minnesota returned to Bolivar Heights at Harpers Ferry. It was there that Colonel Sully was promoted to brigadier vice Gorman who was promoted and sent west to fight Indians in what was called the Dakota War. George Morgan became the new regimental commander.

At Bolivar Heights, many of the sick, wounded and the prisoners from the Peninsular Campaign returned to the Regiment. But this increase was offset when the Regiment was opened to recruiters from the Regular Army, who siphoned off 100 enlisted men to fill various billets in the national army.

It stands to reason that the First would fight itself to oblivion without a replacement system that could make up its losses. This was true for all regiments on both sidees, and especially for the rebel army which could only recruit from a much smaller population. The usual approach was to send a recruiting party to the home state and solicit recruits for the regiment, but this did not produce the desired results, because it was more profitable for potential recruits to take the large bounty offered by the State to enter a new regiment, than it was to enter a battered regiment.

The benefit to the Regiment was that it would enter each battle with all veterans, who knew how to handle themselves properly in combat, and were more effective with smaller companies than the large thousand-man regiments of inexperienced troops in the pipeline to combat.

Rebel recruiters had the same trouble, but they did not have the manpoweor pool from which to draw more men. It did expand the draft age, but got no relief from it. It also voided the terms of service to keep men in service for the duration. Finally, there was the problem of mass desertions, which kept the Provost Marshall's people stymied in the last year of the war. At the end, the Union army totalled slighty more than one million versus the Confederate's none.

Chapter Six

Fredericksburg: "We had a hell of a time, didn't we?"

After Antietam, Little Mac went back to his old dawdling ways, stretching the fatherly patience of President Lincoln right up to, but not including 7 November, when the president sacked him. Lincoln gave General Ambrose Burnside a chance to accelerate the Army of the Potomac towards the decisive victory that would close the Rebellion.

More than half of the Minnesota First's line officers tended their resignations, so beloved was McClellan by the troops. But calmer heads prevailed and the tenders were withdrawn. November 10th, the day McClellan bid farewell to his troops, saw troop morale at its lowest.

General Burnside tried to refuse the command: "I am not competent to command such a large army as this."

President Lincoln should have heeded this general's opinion of himself, but Lincoln was desperate: he persuaded Burnside to replace General McClellan.

Burnside wasn't much faster afoot than McClellan had been. Headquartered at Warrenton, Burnside spent ten days consolidating the units of his new command into three 'Grand Divisions': the Right, the Center and the Left.

On 15 November 1862, he moved the Army back to Falmouth, VA, on the south bank of the Rappahannock opposite Fredericksburg, a distance of 30 miles.

Burnside's plan was to spend the winter at Fredericksburg and use it as a base of operations against Richmond. Before he could operate against Richmond he had to seize Fredericksburg. The city was occupied by four Mississippi companies of Barksdale's Brigade, Lewis's Virginia Artillery and Ball's 15th Virginia Cavalry.

General Sumner wanted to move quickly across the Rappahannock to seize Fredericksburg and the heights behind it via two shallow fords above the city. General Burnside overruled him. Instead, he wanted to put his army across the Rapahannock on the pontoons that Washington had promised would arrive at Falmouth at the same time his army arrived. The Grand Divisions concentrated on Falmouth on 20 November, but the pontoons didn't arrive until the 25th. From then until 11 December, Burnside never attempted a crossing. Lee used Burnside's delay to concentrate his army on Fredericksburg: he called in Jackson's corps in from the Valley and Longstreet's in from Culpeper.

One bridge too far

The first part of Burnside's scheme was to cross the swollen river and occupy the city. After nine attempts to bridge the river, Howard's Division finally got across on the night of 11 December and occupied the town. The rest of the Army moved across the river on the 12th. In cold and depressing weather, the men lay all night on their arms. They were scheduled to attack on the morning of the 13th.

Against 20,000 infantry and over 50 cannon, each Union division, in its turn, was thrown against Lee's works on Marye's Heights.

First to attack was General French's Division, 2,800 officers and men. Result: 1,160 casualties.

Next, Hancock's Division. Result: 2,021 casualties out of 4,834 officers and men.

Next came Howard's division (Colonels Owens's and Hall's brigades). Result: Owens's brigade: 258 casualties; Hall's brigade of 800 troops: 515 casualties (64%).

Next: Sturgis's Division of the IX Corps with Ferrero's and Nagel's brigades. Result: 1,007 casualties.

Humphrey's Division followed. Result: 1,020 out of 3,500.

Then came Griffin's Division. Result: another 938 casualties.

Not one Union soldier made it to the Confederate works.

Confederate losses: Hood's division lost 343 and Pickett's a scant 46.

From 11 to 14 December, Burnside traded over 12,000 Union casualties for over 5,000 Confederate ones, an offer hard for Lee to refuse. Every brigade in the II Corps presented itself for target practice on Marye's Heights, all, that is, except Sully's brigade. It was last in line but kept out of the firing line by Sully's brave refusal to murder his own troops. Nevertheless, First Minnesota's casualties were 15 wounded and one man captured, when pickets were recalled.

The Regiment recrossed the Rappahannock the night of 14 December and returned to quarters at Falmouth were it spent the remainder of the winter. From blood-march to mud-march.

Burnside learned that there is a difference between the theory of leadership and the actual practice of leadership in war as opposed to peacetime maneuvers or war games. Burnside knew that leadership at the army level required both tactical and strategic expertise. Strategic expertise is not a prerequisite to exercising command and control at corps and lower levels. Tactics were simply the methods used by armies: the standard operating procedures by which an army conducts itself in combat operations using the weaponry at hand.

Tactics were as far as the Army of the United States went. The United States Military Academy at West Point was essentially a liberal arts college that issued degrees in engineering. Cadets were taught painting, philosophy, ethics, mathematics, and physics. One of the few military courses was tactics. There was no course in strategy, which was sketchily covered in tactics, almost as an oversight because the country did not support an army large enough to have strategic aims, nor did it have a general staff that could develop such plans.

Having beaten the British in the Revolution, the Federal government was scarcely put to defend itself during the War of 1812, which saw the British burn Washington, a war that was won at New Orleans by Andrew Jackson and a citizens army.

Again, in the Mexican War, the only soldier who had a strategic grasp of what tactics were needed to beat Santa Ana was Winfield Scott, and it was his strategy of naval operations against the East coast, the Mississippi, and the Gulf of Mexico, while squeezing the Confederacy by military operations from the North (Grant and company) that beat the Confederacy.

This lack of a strategic sense worked against Burnside. Given control of the Army of the Potomac, he had no real sense about how he was to command and control so large a force. Instead of using the old organization, he killed time by reorganizing the army into three 'Grand Divisions.' But that was corps commander thinking: "I can handle three divisions in a corps, so if I convert this army into divisions, I should be able to do the job."

What Burnside did at Fredericksburg was akin to what the naval people call "Crossing the T" only he let the rebels do it to him. "Crossing the T" means that one fleet in line manages to move across an enemy fleet in line to form a T. The fleet forming the cross arm is able to direct fire from all its guns at the head of the oncoming enemy and so destroy it one ship at a time; without receiving return fire from its opponent. At Fredericksburg, the rebels formed the cross arm of the T on Marye's Heights, while Burnside sent his divisions in single file where they received devastating enfilade fire from both flanks and the center of the enemy line.

But when it was over, the morale of the Union army hadn't fallen very much: One of the survivors was heard to tell his buddy: "We had a hell of a time, didn't we?"

Chapter Seven

Hooker's Hook Unhooked

On 26 January 1863, Fighting Joe Hooker succeeded Burnside to the command of the Army of the Potomac. One of his first acts was to reorganize the Army into a series of corps, each recognizable by unique corps and division badges. The II Corps badge was a trefoil or cloverleaf design, and for the 2nd Division, in which the Minnesota First was mustered, their cloth badge was white to be worn on the cap.

Hooker's plan: to swing a large part of his army behind Lee's force at Fredericksburg and use the remainder to fix Lee in position, was begun on 27 April 1864.

The First Minnesota's camp was within sight of rebels, so it was decided to leave them and their division in place so as not to tip of the rebels that something was up.

Sergeant Walker noted: *"Troops are moving, hard to tell which way they go—this forenoon we see troops filing to the right, and this afternoon they return and go to the left."*

The next day he observed: *"Some firinig today, both up and down the river. Most of the troops have left (with the exception of our division) makes the place look deserted and lonely."*

It appeared Hooker's campaign was not getting off on the right foot. While the rest of the army moved, one of the First Minnesota's sister regiments started a bit of a rebellion themselves, which was quickly sorted out. Sergeant Henry Taylor noted it this way.

"About 100 of the 34th NY Vols claim that their terms (2 years) expires today, and they refuse to do duty. Gens Sully and Gibbons call out the remainder of the regiment, also the 15th Mass, and placed the mutineeers under guard—guns loaded. Gen Gibbons made a speach to them, telling them that they had better return to duty, as the U S Government would not recognize their service until they were sworn into the U S Service. General Gibbon told them he had authority from Gen Hooker to shoot everyone if they did not return to duty. Then they gave three cheers for Gen Cibbon, and returned to duty."

Hooker's plan would have succeeded, if Hooker hadn't lost his nerve that first day, and if General O O Howard had payed attention to the threat to his flank, which was rolled up like an old carpet by Jackson's attack. This took the momentum out of Hooker.

Jackson's attack permitted Lee to support the men Sedgwick's VI Corps had ejected from Fredericksburg. Lee's operational genius had once more baffled and befuddled the brains of the army whose main body was as good at retreating as Lee's was at advancing. By the 4th it was all over, and everybody but the dead and wounded returned to square one.

The First Minnesota Regiment did not fight at Chancellorsville, but spent its time at Fredericksburg where it lost nine men wounded. Captain Bruce of F Company, with 25 skirmishers, led the VI Corps assault up and over Marye's Heights.

Hooker gave up 17,000 in killed, wounded and missing to Lee's 13,000.

Within 30 days, Lee would work up enough of an army to again invade the North. Hooker would follow him, but would succumb to McClellan's syndrome and give up his job three days before the battle he just might have won.

In fairness to Hooker, he might have recovered from Chancellorsville had he not received a concussion when a cannon ball struck his headquarters building, dropping a beam on his head. He had stomach for the fight, but not brains for the fight. He was to recover and do good work in the west

At Fredericksburg and at Chancellorsville, Lee was unable to exploit his initial advantage over the Union army because he did not have the means to pursue a beaten army. It was Bull Run all over again, and every single battle in between.

Logistics superiority means not only the ability to get the materiel to the human gun platforms doing the shooting, it means having enough gun platforms to suppress the enemy, and to make good all losses. Lee lost the equivalent of 13 regiments at Chancellorsville versus 17 regiments for the Blues. Neither the Confederate draft system nor their commissary system could ever make up the losses, nor could they keep their armies properly equipped and fed. Morale surrenders to an empty belly, and the attack comes to a halt at the full haversacks in the enemy camp. It would take Lee almost two months to get the ANV back in shape for the next battle. On paper all armies look invincible, but, in reality, an army that has to get its footwear from the corpses of its enemy is a doomed army.

Farewell to Stonewall

Chancellorsville cost Lee his best corps commander, Stonewall Jackson, wounded by friendly fire, and carried away by pneumonia, after his arm was amputated. His men never fought as well again.

Chapter Eight

From the Virginia Reel to the Pennsylvania Polka

Spring fever

WHILE FIGHTING JOE Hooker recovered from the blow to the head he received at Chancellorsville, the Minnesota 1st went about its military routines at Falmouth, below the Stacy House, under the enemy guns on Marye's Heights half a mile away, with rebel infantry camped across the river.

Spring was in the air: the military sweat of future battles floated through the company streets mixed with the scent of honeysuckle and roses. The men carried out their daily routines and tried to put the last battle behind them. The Chancellorsville-Fredericksburg battle had cost the regiment nine men wounded. What really bothered them was that the Sioux uprising of the previous August had cost the lives of over 1,000 civilians, mostly women and children, and that their presence in Virginia had denuded Minnesota of manpower which might have saved those lives. Realizing that steps were being taken to suppress the Indians and effect the release of all captives, the men of the First Minnesota Regiment maintained their discipline, and reduced the harsh realities of war by whittling small boats of juniper and cedar to conduct maritime trade with rebel pickets on the winning side of the Rappahannock: tobacco, sugar, coffee, and other sundries passed between them.

Spring was barely three weeks old when there was a change of command. Colonel Morgan resigned (ill health) and William Colvill became colonel in his place.

Charles Adams became lieutenant-colonel, and Mark Downie rose in rank to major.

The Minnesotans held a parade for General Sully, who was given a command in Minnesota to fight the Sioux. As a small token of their esteem, the boys bought him a ceremonial sword worth a thousand dollars. Lochren listed Sully as the best loved of all their colonels. He was brave, capable, playful, humorous, and he exhibited every confidence that his troops would act honorably and conduct themselves like men. They never disappointed him.

It was a case of "all quiet on the Rappahannock", until 6 June, when General Hooker broke free of the spell that had frozen his brain. He pushed Sedgwick's VI Corps across the river at Franklin's old crossing, about two miles below the regimental camp ground. Sedgwick's crossing was not contested with much enthusiasm, and he was able to secure a bridgehead on the rebel side of the river. The peace of the Minnesotans was not disturbed.

Then, after this flurry of activity, Hooker went back to sleep.

Quiet reigned once more along the Rappahannock's shores.

General Darius Couch of II Corps went to the newly created Department of the Susquehanna.

The II Corps went to General Winfield Scott Hancock, he whom McClellan had called "superb".

William Harrow, a brigadier of no mean talent, assumed command of Sully's 1st Brigade. Slowly, as if by some mysterious process of evolution, the real leaders of the Army of the Potomac took command. It seemed to be the reverse of the usual process of good leaders giving way to bad leaders as a war progressed. The next campaign might just be a little different.

On 9 June, the First Minnesota Regiment paraded to the railhead to shout farewells to their comrades of the 34th New York, homeward bound after two solid years of service. The 34th was about as large in numbers as the Minnesota Regiment, and a lot of the boys from the North Woods wondered how many coaches they would fill in '64 when their service ended. Yes, it would be a slightly different campaign without the 34th New York, and the 30,000 or so other veterans who would leave the Army that spring—slightly different, indeed.

Critique for the Blue and the Gray

While Hooker dawdled on his side of the Rappahannock, Lee was quietly building up his army for another invasion of the North. His army, too, had aged, had suffered from death, desertion, and disease. Worst of all, Lee had lost the mighty Stonewall Jackson, and hundreds of brave and experienced officers. He was able to beef up his rosters to 75,000 men but most of what he would take with him were not, and never would be, the same as the men he had lost in '61 and '62. In a way, Lee fought his army like a good champion plays chess. He developed his pieces rapidly, concentrated them at his enemy's weak points, and tried to end it all with a killing check. Lee's opening and middle games were superb, but for all his masterful play, he could not checkmate his foe because, after every gambit, the Army of the Potomac, though gaining nothing in a positional sense, came out of the exchange the stronger of the two in material. It was a game in which, for every piece removed by Lee, two more were put on the board for the Blues; the reverse was true for him: he could never quite get to the end game.

It was this preponderance in men and material that, handled properly by the Union command, would bring about Lee's eventual collapse. The attrition rate could not be balanced, in the end game, by the best play he had to offer.

Leadership manuals hold a general responsible for the basic comforts of his troops, that is, it is his job to see that they are issued good rations, kept healthy, clothed, and rested properly, whenever possible. One of Lee's defects as a general was that he did not take the necessary pains required to provide the basic needs of his soldiers, and he rarely inspected their camps. His army had to improvise, beg, borrow, steal, and live off the pickings of the Union armies. The truth of the matter is that pickings do not go very far, stomachs and shoes being what they are. Lee's men stripped the dead, both Union and Confederate, of their shoes, clothing, rations, money and equipment. D S Freeman mentions that the battle of Gettysburg was brought about because Confederate troops were drawn there by thoughts of boots and brogans. It was estimated that for Union troops a pair of shoes lasted two months, a uniform four months, and that the demands and usage of battle strained even the Union Supply Corps. After Antietam, Meade reported that many of his troops were barefooted, although that condition did not last long.

In the long run, an army that is always hungry, always in need of shoes and clothing, fights with fifty percent of its morale missing, the kind of morale it walks on, and drops in its frying pans. Getting wounded or killed was a one-shot operation, but an empty stomach is a special kind of wound, bloodless, but more hurtful, more disabling, and more persistent than any wound we care to name. Quite possibly this desire to have something to eat three times a day is what caused the high desertion rate in the rebel armies; and having to shoot oneself "a pair of shoes" did not come without cost either.

Something more than a river separated the two armies. The rebel camp was spread out and disordered like a hobo jungle, a private domain into which Lee seldom went. The Federal camp was laid out in an orderly fashion, with regular company streets, arbored, and kept clean. The rebels rarely knew when they would get rations; the Federals had both the quantity and quality (comparatively speaking) of rations issued at dependable intervals. The Confederates wore a motley array of uniforms while the Federals had standard uniforms and two pairs of good shoes. Finally, in the matter of armaments and medicines, the rebels were constantly in short supply, while the Union troops wallowed in the armaments of war and the medicines of healing.

What of fighting qualities? Was the rebel trooper worth three Union soldiers? Hardly. What Southern regiment fought a better fight against odds than Keenan's 8th Pennsylvania, a fight which saw 80 per cent of his 400 men fall, wounded and dead? Keenan said, "This will kill us, but we'll do it".

They did, and they died, but they held Jackson up long enough to permit the unlimbering of artillery reserves that blasted Jackson's troops to a standstill.

In that same battle, Chancellorsville, Jackson's own brigade balked twice before they assaulted Slocum's line. Only a personal appeal from General Dick Anderson got them moving, only to be repulsed. Their performance was not something Stonewall would have gloried in.

An analysis of the confederate army, and the battles it won, will show that it was usually able to apply, in its attacks, a superior force that eventually pushed a brave but inferior number of Union troops before it. Lee, as a commander, had learned the principles of war, and used his army to apply them. He implemented the natural bravery of his men, which led to the several successes they enjoyed. Lee gave his men success by using them properly, and it was those successes that made them feel superior to the men they fought.

The Boys in Blue knew they were as good as, if not better, than the men they fought, but the effect Lee's winning style had on their leaders—a failure of nerve—kept them from victories they might have won. McClellan knew how to act, but was reluctant to act—he kept stopping himself; Burnside did not know how to act, and Hooker, who acted as if he knew how to act, ceased acting at the critical moment. They were simply not as good as the men they commanded and the men they faced, although just as brave.

In short, Lee was worth any number of Union generals, in technique, in audacity, and in generalship; the army he commanded was not, man for man, better than the Army of the Potomac. Gettysburg was to bear that out.

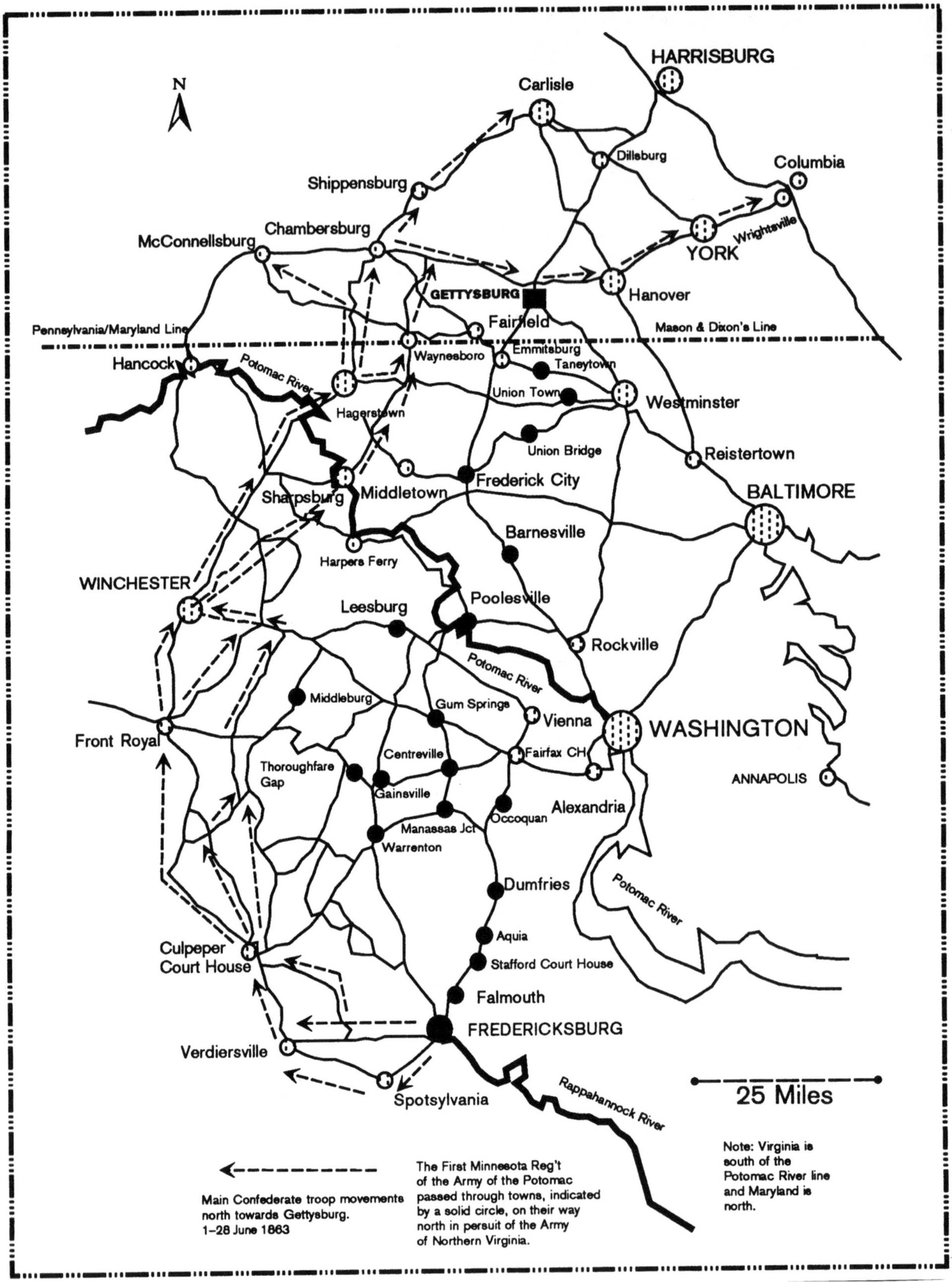
N
HARRISBURG
Carlisle
Dillsburg
Columbia
Shippensburg
Chambersburg
McConnellsburg
YORK
Wrightsville
Hanover
GETTYSBURG
Fairfield
Mason & Dixon's Line
Pennsylvania/Maryland Line
Hancock
Potomac River
Waynesboro
Emmitsburg
Taneytown
Union Town
Westminster
Hagerstown
Union Bridge
Reistertown
Sharpsburg
Middletown
Frederick City
BALTIMORE
Barnesville
Harpers Ferry
WINCHESTER
Leesburg
Poolesville
Rockville
Potomac River
Middleburg
Gum Springs
Vienna
WASHINGTON
Front Royal
Centreville
Fairfax CH
Thoroughfare Gap
Gainsville
ANNAPOLIS
Alexandria
Occoquan
Manassas Jct
Warrenton
Dumfries
Potomac River
Aquia
Stafford Court House
Culpeper Court House
Falmouth
FREDERICKSBURG
Verdiersville
Spotsylvania
Rappahannock River
25 Miles
Main Confederate troop movements north towards Gettysburg. 1–28 June 1863
The First Minnesota Reg't of the Army of the Potomac passed through towns, indicated by a solid circle, on their way north in persuit of the Army of Northern Virginia.
Note: Virginia is south of the Potomac River line and Maryland is north.

Chapter Nine

Getting There Is Half the Fun

General Hooker frittered May away with skirmishes and cavalry actions. He did nothing with VI Corps on Lee's side of the river, and somehow got the notion that Lee would do nothing on his side of the river, but he was wrong once again.

In June, Lee:

1. began moving around Hooker's right, screened by Stuart's horse, reported active in the Shenandoah, 12 June;

2. had Ewell swamp Milroy's weary 12,000 men at Winchester, forcing him and 2,000 survivors back on Harpers Ferry; and

3. moved away from Fredericksburg, slowly.

President Lincoln questioned Hooker: "If the head of Lee's Army is at Winchester and the tail at Fredericksburg, the animal must be thin somewhere. Could you not break him?"

Hooker did not think so. His vision was clouded by the dust raised by Confederate cavalry. He cried, like General McClellan, for more reinforcements.

Union cavalry, led by young lions like Buford, Custer, Gregg, and Kilpatrick, had managed to keep the rebels out of the Blue Ridge passes, clouding Lee's notions about the location of Hooker and company. He thought them all to be at Fredericksburg, but Hooker had a corps at Frederick, Maryland and another closer to Washington.

On 13 June, Hooker pulled Sedgwick out of Fredericksburg.

On 14 June he was wide awake and put his Army in motion. The First Minnesota was rear guard to this array with which they marched five miles, only to be recalled to Falmouth to do a night's picket duty. It was march and countermarch.

At first light on 15 June the pickets were called in; the First marched to and halted at Stafford Court House. At 2pm the men fell in, resuming the march under a hot, merciless sun. Lochren reported that many men succumbed to the heat. The Regiment crossed Acquia Creek, marched several miles and camped for the day.

On the 16th at 3am, the Minnesotans resumed their march. They stopped for breakfast at 7am at Dumfries. By 6pm, the men had crossed the Occoquan, an extension of Bull Run, and bivouacked on the north bank.

On 17 June, the Regiment reached Sangster's Station on the Orange and Alexandria line. Several men dropped out from sunstroke and heat prostration.

On the 19th, the Regiment moved south toward Centreville.

There was a riot on 20 June when troopers from the First Minnesota, and other regiments got into a hassle with the sutler of the 9th Massachusetts Battery. The argument ended with the sacking of the sutler's tent. To stabilize things, a half-battery of artillery was run out but captured by the aroused troopers who rolled the field pieces down a hill, dispersing rapidly.

Before the Provost Marshall could act, the Army of the Potomac was put in motion. That same day, the First Minnesota crossed the old Bull Run battlefield en route to Gainesville.

On the 21st, they marched to Thoroughfare Gap, north of Gainesville. They remained there until 25 June guarding the pass and the trains moving north through it. On the forenoon of that day, the Second

Division, as rear guard of the army, moved toward Haymarket on the report that Stuart's horsemen were moving on the long wagon trains that formed the tail of the army.

At Haymarket, the rebel horsemen unlimbered a battery, fired enough rounds to kill several men in the division, wound two men in the Minnesota Regiment, and shoot Colonel Colvill's horse out from under him. Lochren writes that the panic and flight of the noncombatants: doctors, chaplains, sutlers, and servants gave the combat infantrymen a good laugh as they formed a skirmish line, advanced on the guns, and drove the rebels off. They finished the day with a march of 22 miles to Gum Springs.

By noon of the 26th, the Minnesota First crossed the Potomac at Edwards Ferry, with the rest of the army, to camp near its old bivouac of October '61. General Hooker was concentrating his army on Frederick, Maryland, not too slowly at that.

By 28 June, the Minnesotans were at the Monocacy, overlooking Frederick, where Dame Barbara Fritchie had put Stonewall to shame the year before for shooting at the old flag. "Shoot if you must, this old gray head, but spare your country's flag," she said.

On this day, too, Fighting Joe Hooker, miffed with Lincoln for not sending him the Harpers Ferry garrison, resigned command of the Army of the Potomac. Yet, he did not state that as the reason for his resignation:

"My original instructions require me to cover Harper's Ferry and Washington. I have now imposed upon me, in addition, an enemy in my front of more than my number. I beg to be understood, respectfully but firmly, that I am unable to comply with the means at my disposal, and I earnestly request that I may at once be relieved from the position I occupy."

President Lincoln accepted his resignation and appointed General George Meade. He would have just three days to get control of the army before Gettysburg. Hooker tried to gain a subordinate position to General Meade. Lincoln wanted to grant his wish, but Meade blocked that. Later, Hooker was sent to Chattanooga after Chickamauga.

XI Corps + XII Corps = XX Corps

Hooker was later given command of the XX Corps (formed by consolidating the XI and XII Corps). He untarnished his reputation at the Battle of Lookout Mountain, and during the Atlanta Campaign.

General Meade was not charismatic like McClellan, or a braggart like Hooker, but a simple working general who was to give the Potomac Army the decisive leadership it had suffered two years to get, and a victory that would have General Lee admit, "It was all my fault this time."

General Meade tried to decline the command, feeling that Reynolds was better able to lead the Army. The army expected Reynolds to be given command, as did Reynolds himself, but when Meade was selected, Reynolds personally gave his loyalty to Meade and Meade then took the job.

The duty soldier

Meade came out of West Point (1835), served in the Seminole and the Mexican Wars, came into the Civil War as a brigadier; was wounded (hip and knee) at White Oak Swamp, commanded Reynold's outfit at South Mountain, and led V Corps at Fredericksburg, and at Chancellorsville.

For the first time, the Army of the Potomac was lead by a general who was ready to fight it properly.

June 29th, and with it, a 31-mile march in fierce heat to Uniontown, on the Pennsylvania line. There was contact with enemy pickets—the sweat of battle was in the air.

On 30 June, the Regiment rested. Its only activity was to muster its thin companies for Pay Call. The June muster showed 27 officers and 358 men present for duty, a total of 383. A ball was organized by the citizens of the town, and revellers from the First were up to the early hours.

We did it before; we can do it again

June was at an end. It had been a hot month, made terrible by long marches, sunstroke, riots, and skirmishes, but it had brought the troops out of Virginia, the scene of so many of its defeats, and into the North, again, where it had previously turned the rebels away at Antietam.

For the Minnesota men, June had been alive with the rumor that McClellan, yesterday's warrior-god, would return to head the army vice Hooker who was wearing out his welcome by the same reluctance and slowness to battle which had tumbled "Little Mac," who would have taken six months to get the men out of Fredericksburg, was still remembered fondly by this army. With Meade's appointment, Minnesota joy was short-lived.

No time for wet feet

June was the month in which the Regiment saw Colonel Colvill placed under arrest by II Corp Inspector-General Morgan. The charge: disobedience. The specification: allowing his men to cross a small stream on planks when they had been ordered to wade across. Colvill saw no reason why his men should cripple their feet by marching in wet brogans. The reason for Morgan's action: he had been stoutly razzed by the 15th Massachusetts, and mistook the Minnesotans for the men from New England.

These boots were made for marching

June ended with the Minnesota First at Uniontown, 17 miles from the crossroads-town of Gettysburg towards which the Grey army had been lured in search of shoes, food, and forage, with the Blue army in pursuit. The II Corps, and the Minnesota First, as an articulate part of that corps, brought up the rear.

On the First Day of battle

The Battle of Gettysburg began on 1 July, north and west of the town with the 1st Cavalry Division, (Devin and Gamble's brigades of General Buford) contesting the rebel advance of Heth's and Pender's Divisions of A P Hill's Corps—about 20,000 men and 92 cannon. Buford gave ground slowly, making the rebels fight for the substance of their advance. Buford was first reinforced by Wadsworth's Division of Reynolds's I Corps, then by Doubleday's and Robertson's Divisions, whose black-hatted Iron Brigade went surging in with cheers and fury. General Oliver Otis Howard's unlucky XIth Corps came into line north of Gettysburg where it made good progress against Ewell's Corps until Jubal Early's rogues flanked him on the right. That movement compromised the whole Union front. It looked like the same old story, as the reeling Union line dropped back through the town seeking safety on the high ground south of it. Hancock, coming on the scene, assumed command, and decided to construct a Union battle line on the hook-shaped ridge that dominated the field. It went by the name Cemetery Ridge. Generals Hill and Ewell, finally bought to a standstill, decided to wait for orders from Lee, and broke the action off at nightfall.

III + XII = 2 Corps

Night saw the arrival of Slocum's XII and Sickles's III Corps, making the Federal line thick and heavy with the strength of four corps. Missing: V Corps (Sykes) VI Corps (Sedgwick) and the rear guard, Hancock's II Corps.

The Union Army was pulling itself taut rather smartly in the shape of a fishhook on which the Confederates had just got their first nibble.

The pulsing sounds of battle, beating artillery, and firm ripples of musketry, reached the Minnesota campground at Uniontown, seventeen miles distant. Battle sounds, then silence, then a restless rising from the hot ground as the men responded to marching orders. A camp hastily broken up, fires doused, companies falling in, names being called, equipment adjusted, horses mounted, sergeants shouting orders, and the movement towards Gettysburg begun. Battle fever glazed the eyes of men, and pulses quickened. The II Corps moved towards Gettysburg. By 4pm they met, as Lochren described it, *"the crowd of cowards and camp followers, fleeing in terror, with their frightened tales of utter defeat and rout. As most of the soldiers wore the crescent badge of the Eleventh Corps, which was held in little respect since Chancellorsville, they received taunts and jeers from the sturdy veterans of the II Corps."*

Shortly after II Corps passed Taneytown, a small town about three and a half miles south of Gettysburg, a halt was called. It was 8pm, and the battle slackened to whisperings of picket fire. The Minnesota First threw out a strong picket line, and barricaded itself against night attack.

The Arena of Time

Time was running out for the Minnesota infantry. Two years of battle had reduced the Regiment by about 600 effectives. Of the 1,042 mustered in at Fort Snelling in the spring of 1861, slightly less than 400 riflemen were left to face the music. In that same corps, there were new regiments a thousand strong, bright with new equipment, bright with young faces, which reminded the Minnesotans of how they had looked when their regiment was born, reminded them of 600 missing buddies, whose imprint marked the memory and the bearing of the 385 survivors, who in turn would remind the new regiments, new to combat, that they were the 'regiment with the reputation' and would fight for that reputation to the last man.

There were several thousand volunteer regiments raised by both sides, and hundreds had combat records similar to that of the Minnesota First. Many served for three years and suffered 50% or more in casualties and they were mostly young men in the 17 to 25 age group raised on the farm.

The regimentals had greater cohesion, were less prone to surrender or desert. Coming from small towns in the state of origin, they took greater pride in their regiment. The First Regiment had one deserter, but his name never showed up in state documents.

The regiment, in short, was a kinship group. It could look forward to going home together with their buddies and being able to continue army friendships in civilian life. "Time will take us through the roughest day," as Shakespeare put it, but 2 and 3 July were to be Minnesota's roughest days and Time took very few of the boys through it.

Chapter Ten

You can't win them all, Bobby Lee

BATTLE-EVE CAME for the Minnesota First, older by some 700 days, poorer by the loss of so many men, but richer in courage and bravery and memory, at Taneytown. They were battle-hardened riflemen in faded blue uniforms, feet encased in march-broken shoes, bodies etched by the sweat of a 31-mile march. Some stretched out on ground cloths, packs for head rests, trying to sleep, while others oiled their Springfield rifles and prepared for tomorrow. Tomorrow? Who among them could read tomorrow in the embers of the fading night?

On the Second Day of battle

On 2 July at 3am the bugles sounded reveille: early morning stirrings of men rolling blankets, making packs, washing, putting the coffee to boil, answering to names called out in the darkness. For many of the men, the bugles would sound reveille for the last time. Isaac Lyman Taylor, of E company, would make his last diary entry and pass out of the "arena of time" as he called it, without having his diary fall into "secesh" hands.

He would not be alone.

Slowly, with ancient routine, the Regiment got to its feet. There was still time to smell bacon, taste bitter coffee, choke on hardtack, unlimber stiff muscles, write a letter, smoke a pipe, crack a joke, sing a song, laugh, shout, cry, reminisce, pray, and breathe wooded air, but there was no way to get to the future but by marching into it at Gettysburg. For many the future stopped at the apex formed by the Emmittsburg and the Taneytown Roads that formed a huge arrowhead whose tip pierced the heart of Gettysburg.

It was Thursday and, by 4am, the Minnesota First had its feet on the Taneytown Road. They marched north into the Union line at Cemetery ridge.

At 5.45am John Gibbon, Second Division commander, read an order to the Minnesotans informing them they were about to fight the most important battle of the war, and that any man leaving the ranks would be summarily shot.

Colonel Colvill was released from arrest and restored to command vice Adams; they now had everything for the fight.

The Second Corps line

There were three divisions in the II Corps: Caldwell's 1st, Gibbon's 2nd; and Hay's 3rd, which lined up south to north in the order named on the line described below.

General Gibbon, who was to command the II Corps, describes, the ground occupied by that body of infantry on 2 July:

"...the line of the 2nd AC extended from a short distance to the left of Cemetery Hill, in a curved line along the brow of the hill, and turning Southward at the clump of Oak and Chestnut trees, where Woodruff's Battery, 1st Artillery was placed. The line extended along a low stone wall until this reached a point where it made a right angle to the front, and say fifty yards to the front of that the fence joined on to another, part stone, part rails, along which the line was prolonged to the left.

"In this angle, formed by the fence, and a short distance to the left of the turn in the wall, was a clump of trees with thick underbrush and briar beneath.

"From the highest point on the right of my Division, the ridge gradually falls off to the left, until it reaches its lowest point at a spring and a little piece of marshy ground beyond which it begins to rise again in the direction of Round Top, the intervening space being rocky

and partially covered with timber.

"In front of my Division, the ground gently sloped off toward the Emmitsburg Road, which ran obliquely across my front and, after passing the Codori House about 100 yards in front of my center, could be seen gently rising over the sloping hills beyond, till it disappeared behind what was afterwards known as the Peach Orchard. The Emmitsburg Road had on each side of it a strong post and rail fence, and beyond it the gently undulating ground stretched away a mile, perhaps, to a ridge fringed with timber where the enemy had his batteries, and where his line of battle was supposed to be."

Division and brigade lineup

The II Corps of Hancock consisted of three divisions: Caldwell's 1st, Gibbon's 2nd, and Hays's 3rd.

Each division contained three or four brigades. Caldwell's Division consisted of Cross's 1st, Kelly's 2nd, Zook's 3rd and Brookes's 4th brigades.

Gibbon's Division consisted of Harrow's 1st, Webb's 2nd and Hall's 3rd brigades.

Hays's Division consisted of Carroll's 1st, Smyth's 2nd and Millard's 3rd brigades.

Harrow's regiments

Harrow's 1st brigade consisted of the 1st Minnesota, the 15th Massachusetts, the 82nd New York, each of ten companies.

II Corps deployment

On 2 July the II Corps deployed on Cemetery Ridge, facing Seminary Ridge, one mile west of the town. The divisions of the Corps were in line from north to south, from Ziegler's grove to the Weickert house, a front of about 5,400 feet, occupied by about 6,500 men.

General Gibbon's aide, Frank Haskell, stated that the II Corps formation "was in line by brigade in column, the brigades in column by regiments, with 40 paces interval between regimental lines."

The normal line of battle consisted of four common deployed lines, each of two ranks of men, and a little more than a third was in reserve.

The reserves were formed up about 150 paces in rear of the main line of resistance.

XI Corps deployment

The XI Corps of Howard extended the line on Hancock's right, in a large semicircle, tapering off east of town on Culp's Hill.

III Corps deployment

The III Corps (Sickles), composed of Birney's 1st, and Humphrey's 2nd divisions, extended Hancock's line southward, forming the left flank of the Army of the Potomac.

Humphrey's brigades of Carr, Brewster and Burling tied in with Caldwell's left, while Birney's brigades of Ward, Graham, and De Trobriand fell in on Humphrey's line.

The II Corps front before the Sickle's shift was 3,600 feet.

Artillery deployment

According to Haskell, five batteries of artillery, 28 guns, were emplaced as follows:

"Woodruff's Regular, 6–12 pound Napoleons, brass, between the two Brigades in line of the 3rd Division; Arnold's A, 1st Rhode Island, 6–3 inch Parrott's, rifled, and Cushing's Regular, 4–3 inch ordnance, rifled, between the 3rd and 2nd Divisions: Hazard's (commanded during the battle by Lieutenant Brown) B, First Rhode Island, and Rorty's NY, each 6–12 pound Napoleons, brass, between the 2nd and 1st."

Lee's deployment

Opposite the Union array, stretched for six miles, was the Army of Northern Virginia, commanded by Robert E Lee, who had reorganized his divisions into three army corps: First (Longstreet) Second (Ewell) and Third Corps (A P Hill). As a result of the action of the first day, these corps were deployed from north to south, in line, as follows: Third Corps, Second Corps and First Corps.

The Army of Northern Virginia held the town of Gettysburg, and was snugly wrapped around Culp's Hill, held by XII Corps of Slocum, supported by I Corps. South of town, the rebels were strung out in a loose line of battle in the woods fronting Seminary Ridge, a mile from and parallel to Cemetery Ridge.

Five o'clock shadows

The First Minnesota Regiment began the day in Division Rear as part of the Corps Reserve.

Captain Coates reported that the battle *"commenced at daylight and raged with fury the entire day. We were under a severe artillery fire, but not actively engaged until about five o'clock P.M. when we were moved to support Battery C, 4th U.S. Artillery. Company F had been detached as skirmishers, Company L as sharpshooters. C Company was detailed to Division Provost Guard, making eight companies, about 265 men, available for duty, counting staff."*

Sickles gets a leg up

To understand what happened to these eight companies, something of the previous fighting must be told.

On 2 July, at about 1pm, General Sickles moved his III Corps forward from Cemetery Ridge, and from Hancock's left, so that Sickle's division of Birney was stretched out between Round Top on the left, and Sherfy's Peach Orchard on the right (about 1/2 mile) connecting with the Emittsburg road.

Peaches without cream

Humphrey's division was strung out an equal distance from the Peach Orchard along the Emmitsburg road, with his unsupported right near the Codori House. Sickles contended that his movement was a justifiable one.

Meade thought otherwise: *"General Sickles, this is in some respects higher ground than that to the rear, but there is still higher in front of you, and if you keep on advancing you will find constantly higher ground all the way to the mountains."*

But before a change could be safely made, the rebels exploited Sickles's new alignment by attack ing it.

In four hours of furious combat, McLaws's and Hood's Divisions of Longstreet smashed Birney, and bent Humphrey's line back from both naked flanks into a horseshoe, which dissolved from the intense pressure.

The collapse of III Corps occurred despite the fact that Caldwell's Division of the II Corps went to Humphrey's aid, and Willard's Brigade of Hays attempted to shore up Birney.

Humphrey saw the attack:

> *"The fire that we went through was hotter in artillery and as destructive as Fredericksburg. It was for a time positively terrific; the troops on my left retired, leaving me to catch it, my left flank being turned all the time. I had to retire, withdrawing my left flank and falling back on open ground under a heavy artillery fire; 20 times did I bring my men to a halt and face about, H—————— and others forcing the men to do it; they had taken my reserve brigade to support others, and a large part of my second line I had to bring to the front and part of it went to others."*

General John Gibbon of the II Corps had seen the action develop against Humphreys: *"Noticing that beyond the Peach Orchard and directly on Humphreys left was a stand of timber, I turned to General Hancock and asked, 'Do you suppose the enemy has anything in that woods?' At that moment Humphreys left came under fire."*

Caldwell was sent forward to help.

A country mile

Francis Walker, Assistant Adjutant-General of the Army of the Potomac saw the situation:

"The position of the Union left centre had now become exceedingly critical. The disaster to Birney had drawn to the extreme left, the whole V Corps and Caldwell's Division of the IInd, leaving a mile destitute of troops. Of this interval, Humphrey's depleted troops could fill but a small part. Upon receipt of the intelligence of the disaster to the III Corps, followed closely by the news that General Sickles had been desperately wounded, General Meade placed General Hancock in command of that Corps, as well as of his own, throwing upon him the responsibility of meeting the emergency thus created.

"There were troops enough in the Federal Army, but could they be brought up in time to prevent McLaws and Anderson from penetration our line, crossing Plum Run, and reaching the Taneytown road?"

Plugging the gap

General Meade, who sent to the I and XII Corps to plug the gap in Union line, wondered, as did Walker, and Hancock, and thousands of others, whether they would arrive in time to stem the rebel advance.

Gibbon did what he could:

"I sent two regiments from my Division: 15th Massachusetts and the 82nd New York out to the Codori House to protect the right of his (Humphrey's) line so that his connection with the main line might not entirely be lost, and later when Humphrey's line began to give way, two other Regiments (42nd N.Y. and 19th Mass) were sent directly to the front to assist in stemming the torrent of retreat.

"The pressure on Humphreys became so great, especially on his left, that the whole line commenced falling back, followed up almost immediately by lines of infantry marching from his left and alongside the Emmitsburg Road. As Humphreys' men came back, I directed the fire of the two batteries in the right of my line, over the heads of Humphreys' men, at the enemy beyond, using, however, only round shot, for fear of bursting shells hurting our own men."

15th Massachusetts moves

Lieutenant Colonel Joslin, 15th Massachusetts, companion regiment to the Minnesota First, had this experience on the Emmitsburg Road:

"Early on the morning of the 2nd, we moved from our place of bivouac in the rear of the First Minnesota, and took our position in close column by Regiments near the battlefield, stacked arms and remained until 4 o'clock in the afternoon, when the enemy opened from their batteries. Colonel Ward who had been in command of the brigade was relieved and took command of the regiment, and moved by order of General Harrow to the front of our batteries, and took position on the right of the 82nd New York, their left resting near a brick house (Codori House) about 200 yards to the front, nothing connecting on our right. Here we built a small breastwork of rails behind the fence, during which time the enemy were being engaged on our left and a rapid picket firing on our front. We remained in this position half an hour, when the pickets were driven in, and the 82nd N.Y. became engaged. Upon the approach of the enemy, their batteries in our rear opened fire with grape and canister, by which we lost a large number killed and wounded.

"At this time the 82nd NY fell back, exposing our left and rear to a deadly fire from the Rebel infantry. Here Colonel Ward received wounds from which he has since died. We now opened a rapid fire, but being left alone could not hold the position but a short time. When we retired in some disorder, being pressed so closely that we lost quite a number prisoners, captured by the enemy. We reformed our line in rear of the batteries, and rejoined the Brigade, which was moved after dark to the front line."

July First had gone to the Confederates; it certainly looked good for them most of the afternoon of the second day.

It was nearing 5pm: Outside of the failure to take Round Top, the rebels had managed to compromise

Sickles's III Corps, making it possible for them to drive straight up the slope, pierce the remnants on Cemetery ridge, cross the Taneytown road, and whip the Army of the Potomac for the umpteenth time, so help them Robert E. Lee.

What could be done to hold off this rising flood of southern infantry?

General Hancock looked around and saw the uncommitted soldiery of the First Minnesota. They had missed the fighting of the First Day, and it looked as though they might be of some use.

The Minnesota Regiment had been moved "from their original position in the rear, to the left of a Battery commanded by Lieutenant Thomas, and stationed on the high ground a short distance to the left of the Division line of battle."

Captain Coates (A company) reported that the First Minnesota's position at Battery C was near the center of the line evacuated by III Corps. There were no other troops near the Minnesotans, and the battery they had been sent to support; they spent their time watching the fight Humphreys and Birney had been waging to their front.

Lochren saw the action between the Peach Orchard and the Trostle House, from his position a half-mile from both places:

"We saw Sickles's men give way before the heavier forces of Longstreet and Hill, and come back, slowly at first, and rallying at short intervals, but at length broken and in utter disorder rushing down the slope, by the Trostle House, across the low ground up the slope on our side, and past our position to the rear, followed by a strong force—the large Brigades of Wilcox and Barksdale, in regular lines, moving steadily in the flush of victory, and firing on the fugitives. They had reached the low ground, and in a few minutes would be at our position at the rear and left flank of our line, which they could roll up, as Jackson did the Eleventh Corps at Chancellorsville."

There it was, all spelled out in blood and blue cloth: Humphreys's line in retreat and Willard's line to the south fought to a standstill, and two brigades of rebels pouring into the gap.

Lochren again:

"There was no organized force nearby to oppose them, except our handful of two hundred and sixty-two men. Most soldiers, in the face of the near advance of such an overpowering force, which had just defeated the better part of an Army Corps, would have caught the panic and joined the retreating masses. But the First Minnesota had never deserted any post, had never retired without orders, and desperate as the situation seemed, and as it was, the Regiment stood firm against whatever might come."

How did the action look to the Confederate commanders involved? Were they inclined to think they had another victory to write home about, a good one that would win end the war, and gain recognition of the Confederacy's right to existence?

Longstreet, another hound for battle, had his corps deployed by early afternoon, and he gave battle at the Round Tops, at the Peach Orchard, and managed to drive Union troops away at all points. His success was not decisive: Union resistance everywhere had been very fierce, and they had counterattacked with fury. Nevertheless, Longstreet felt that the fighting done by his men was "the best three hours fighting ever done by any troops, on any battlefield."

The fighting was far from over.

As part of Lee's battle plan, Dick Anderson's Division of A P Hill, on Longstreet's left, was to move forward in conjunction with any successful movement of Longstreet.

Anderson's Division consisted of four brigades: Wilcox's Alabamans, Perry's Floridians, Wright's Georgians, and the brigade of Carnot Posey. These brigades were deployed from south to north, in the order named, several hundred yards from the Emmitsburg Road. The four brigades had been ordered to advance in echelon, starting with Wilcox, and push what remained of Humphrey's unhappy line before them in a drive on the Union center.

The attack began wrong: Wilcox was forced to move by his left flank because Barksdale's oblique movement through the Peach Orchard interfered with his line of approach. It took some time to get clear of Barksdale, but Wilcox, who had made a name for himself at Salem Church, was able to get his line moving again.

Alabama meets Minnesota

Wilcox on the continuance of his movement:

"Having gained 400 or 500 yards to the left by this flank movement, my command faced by the right flank, and advanced. This forward movement was made in an open field, the ground rising slightly to the Emmitsburg Road, 250 yards distant. Before reaching this road, a line of enemy skirmishers along the fence parallel to the road were encountered and dispersed. The fence being crossed, my men advanced to the road, in which infantry in line of battle were formed. A brisk musketry fight for a few minutes followed, when the enemy gave way, not however till all save two pieces of a Battery that was in the road had been removed. These fell into our hands, the horses having been killed.

"On the far side of the pike, the ground was descending for some 600 or 700 yards. At the bottom of this descent was a narrow valley, through which ran a rocky ravine or stream, fringed with small trees and undergrowth of bushes. Beyond this the ground rose rapidly some 200 yards and upon this ridge were numerous batteries of the enemy. This ridge to my right rose into a succession of higher ridges or spurs of mountains, increasing in height to the right, but to the left gradually descending. When my command crossed the pike and began to descend the slope, they were exposed to an artillery fire from numerous pieces, both from the front and from either flank.

"Before reaching the ravine at the foot of the slope, two lines of infantry were met and broken, and driven pell mell across the ravine. A second battery of six pieces here fell into our hands. From the batteries on the ridge above referred to grape and canister poured into our ranks. This stronghold of the enemy, together with his batteries, were almost won, when still another line of infantry descended the slope in our front at a double quick, to the support of their fleeing comrades and for the defence of the batteries."

The Union infantry reported by Wilcox as being in retreat were no doubt the remnants of Humphreys' line, and the artillery that ripped into Wilcox's Alabama boys were the batteries of the II Corps Gibbon had ordered to fire over the heads of the retiring Blues.

Wilcox continues:

"Seeing this contest so unequal, I dispatched my adjutant to the division commander to ask that support be sent to my men, but none came. Sveral times did this last of the enemy's lines attempt to drive us back, and were as often repulsed. This struggle at the foot of the hill on which were the enemy's batteries, though unequal, was continued for thirty minutes. With a second supporting line, the heights could have been taken. Without support on either my right or my left, my men were withdrawn to prevent their entire destruction or capture. The enemy did not pursue, but my men retired under a heavy artillery fire and returned to their original position in line, bivouacked for the night, pickets being left on the pike."

General Cadmus Marcellus Wilcox, who commanded the brigade, reported a loss of 577 men killed, wounded and missing in the five regiments in his command: the 8th, 9th, loth, 11th and 14th Alabama. His losses were too much to pay for a position on the Emmitsburg Road.

Florida meets Minnesota

Colonel David Lang, who commanded Perry's Florida Brigade (2nd, 5th and 8th regiments), had this to say of his fighting on the Second Day:

"About 5 P.M. I received an order from General Anderson to the effect that General Longstreet was driving back the enemy's left, and that Wilcox would advance whenever General Longstreet's left advanced beyond him. I was ordered to throw forward a strong line of skirmishers and advance with General Wilcox, holding all the ground the enemy yielded.

"At 6 P.M. General Wilcox having begun to advance, I moved forward, being met at the crest of the first hill with a murderous fire of grape, canister and musketry. Moving forward at the double quick, the enemy fell

back beyond their artillery, where they were attempting to rally when we reached the crest of a second hill. Seeing this, the men opened a galling file on them, thickly strewing the ground with their dead and wounded. This threw them into confusion, and when we charged them with a yell, they broke and fled in confusion into the woods and breastworks beyond, leaving four or five pieces of cannon in my front, carrying off, however, most of the horses and limbers. Following them rapidly, I arrived behind a small eminence at the foot of the heights, where the brigade having become scattered, I halted for the purpose of reforming, and allowing the men to catch breath before the final assault on the heights.

"While engaged in reforming here an aide from the right informed me that a heavy force had advanced upon General Wilcox's Brigade, and was forcing it back. At the same time a heavy fire of musketry was poured upon my brigade from the woods 50 yards immediately in front, which was gallantly met, and handsomely replied to by my men. A few moments later, another messenger on my right informed me that General Wilcox had fallen back, and the enemy was some distance in rear of my right flank. Going to the right I discovered that the enemy had passed me more than a 100 yards, and were attempting to surround me. I immediately ordered my men back to the road some three hundred yards to the rear."

Colonel Lang could find no good cover along the road, and was obliged to order his men back to their original position. He also regretted to report that the flag of the 8th Florida had been left behind in the retreat, and that he had suffered 300 killed and wounded out of the thousand who went into the action. Two attacks and two failures. But there was still Wright's and Posey's brigades. Wright's Georgians attacked up the hill, captured some guns at the Angle on Cemetery Ridge, only to be driven off, due to lack of support. Carnot Posey did absolutely nothing on the grounds that he had not been ordered to attack.

How the First Minnesota did it

The ebb and flow of Wilcox's and Lang's Brigades had been witnessed by Captain Martin Maginnis (H Company). The fight looked like this to him:

"At length Sickles' angle was broken. Our troops in front gallantly endeavoring to check the enemy, till fresh battalions of the enemy came down and our gallant boys gave way carrying back their Colors and slightly wounded, and rallying in squads now and then to empty their guns at their pursuers. The rebel batteries poured grape and canister into the retreating groups and their infantry advancing with triumphant yells, showered rapid volleys of leaden balls into the broken ranks.

"Thomas' battery, which had necessarily been silent till these troops had cleared its front, now opened upon the rebel infantry at short range. This turned their attention to an objective point, and soon a group of crimson battle flags were advanced through the smoke toward it, supported on its left, as it was, by the eight companies of the 1st Minnesota—212 officers and men all told.

"Just then Hancock rode up and unable to conceal his agitation asked in almost anguished tones, "Great God, is this all the men we have here?" And turned toward the right, from which was hastening General Alpheus Williams' Division, but still five minutes distant; and before they reached us the enemy would have reached the battery and gained the very heart of the position. Not a hundred yards behind us was the Taneytown road crowded with our wagons and beyond them the hospitals and trains."

Maginnis reported that General Hancock's face lit up with hope. He pointed to the smoke covered masses of the advancing foe, and cried, "Colonel Colvill, advance and take those colors."

Colvill did not question the order of his corps commander. He ordered his companies to fall in for the advance down the slope with one word: "Forward!"

Maginnis describes the attack:

"Their cannon opened on us and shot and shell tore through the ranks and the more deadly Enfield rifles of their infantry centered on us alone. At every step our men fell, yet no one wavers. Every gap is closed up, and bringing down their bayonets the boys press on shoulder to shoulder.

"Five color bearers are shot down, and five times our flag goes proudly forward as before. Within a hundred,

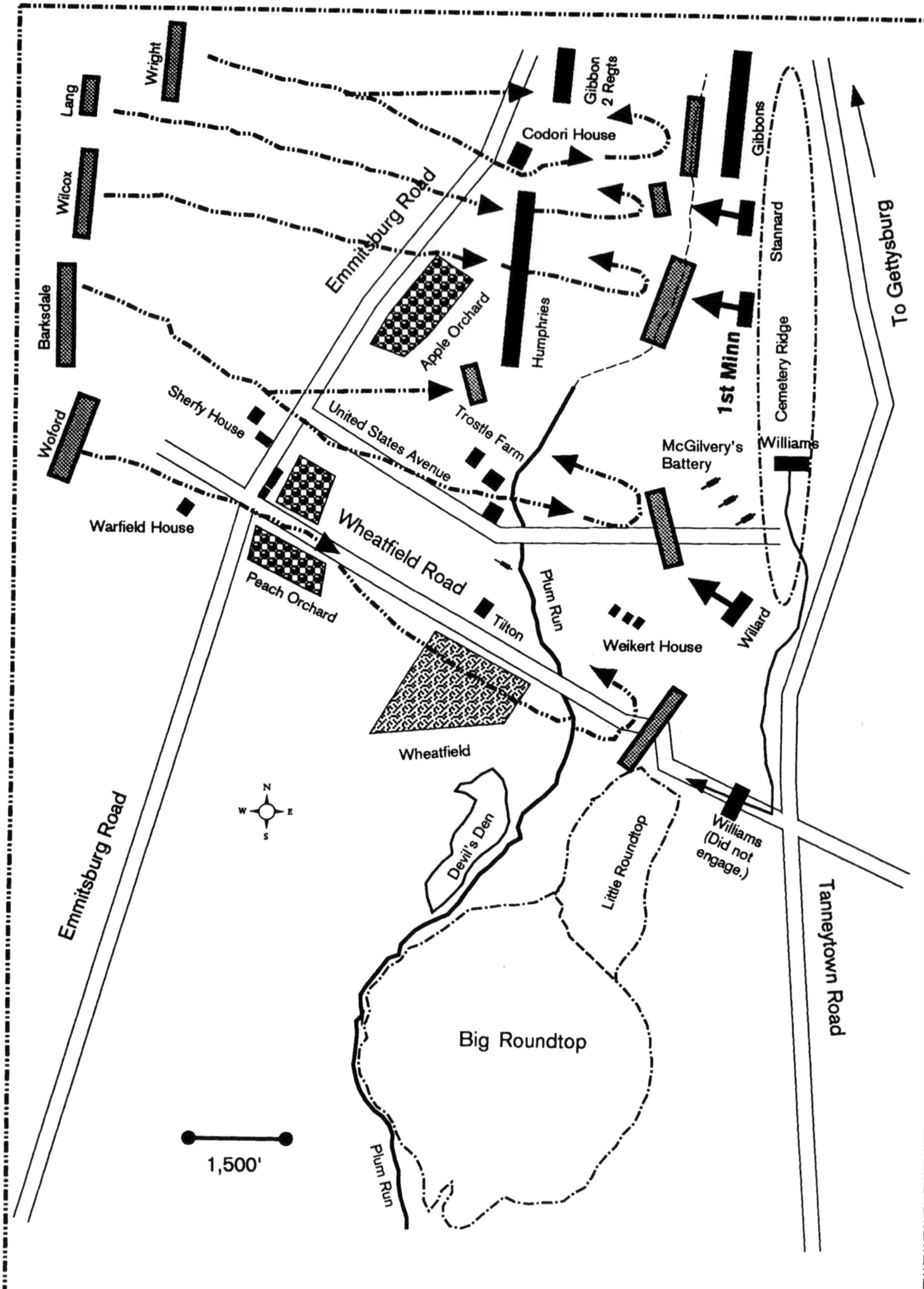

At upper-center The First Minnesota Regiment made its Union-saving charge on 2 July 1863.

within fifty yards of the foe; one quarter of our men are already fallen and yet not one shot has been fired at the enemy, whose foremost ranks consisting of Forney's, Herbert's and other regiments of the Alabama Brigade of Wilcox, and portions of Barksdale's Mississippi Brigade, had lost alignment and became mingled in one advancing mass in their pursuit of the III Corps. Behind them comes the Florida Brigade in alignment. As soon as our movement was noticed the advancing mass stopped, and opened a murderous fire on us not more than fifty yards distant.

"'Charge, men,' rang the orders along the line, and with a wild cheer we ran at them. Their flanks extend around our flanks like waters around a rock. But before us they give way, for we empty our guns with the muzzles at their very hearts, and but little ammunition was wasted at that volley. A perfect swath of men sink to the ground, and their living recoil back on their second and third lines, while the body of many a chivalrous Southerner lies beneath our feet.

"Their supporting lines, confused and excited, wildly commenced firing through the mass in front, slaughtering their own men by hundreds and throwing the whole column into confusion, while their artillery from the rear fired on friend and foe alike."

Lochren, in his account of the charge, said essentially the same thing, varying slightly in the details. It looked like this to him:

"... as we neared their first line, and with leveled bayonets at full speed, we rushed upon it, fortunately, as it was slightly disordered in crossing a dry brook at the foot of the slope. The men were never made who will stand against leveled bayonets coming with such momentum and evident desperation. The first line broke in our front, as we reached it, and rushed back through the second line, stopping the whole advance. We then poured in our first fire, and availing ourselves of such shelter as the low banks of the brook afforded, held the force at bay for a considerable time, until the reserves appeared on the ridge we left. Had the enemy rallied quickly to a countercharge its great numbers would have crushed us in a moment, and we would have made but slight pause in its advance. But the ferocity of our onslaught seemed to paralyze them for a time, and although they poured upon us a terrible and continuous fire from the front and enveloping flanks they kept at respectful distance from our bayonets, until, before the added fire of our fresh reserves, they began to retire, and we were ordered back."

Hancock's comment on the charge of the First Minnesota:

"I ordered those men in there because I saw I must gain five minute's time. Reinforcements were coming on the run, but I knew that before they could reach the threatened point the Confederates, unless checked, would seize the position. I would have ordered that regiment in had I known that every man would be killed. It had to be done, and I was glad to find such a gallant body of men at hand willing to make the terrible sacrifice that the occasion demanded. There is no more gallant deed recorded in history."

Mournful numbers

There is a dispute about the arithmetic of this charge. The tally from the casualty lists in Appendix A show that 42 men were killed and 104 were wounded; 26 later died of their wounds = 172 casualties for 2 July, but Lochren reported that "one man was killed and Sergeant O M Knight of I company was severely wounded by shells from the enemy". This was about noon time, before the charge that evening. Were these men counted as part of the 262 men who charged?

The numbers given below are the historical ones cited in most accounts of this charge.

There were 215 killed, wounded, and later died of wounds reported. With 262 men in the attack, the loss came to 82% of the men engaged. There being 47 men available for another day's battle.

Color-Bearer E B Perkins and two corporals of the Color Guard were shot down.

Captain Muller, E Company, Captain Perriam of K, and Lieutenant Farrar of I Company were shot dead in the charge.

Colonel Colvill was shot through the shoulder and the foot. Patrick Taylor of E Company dragged him from the field.

Lieutenant-Colonel Adams was shot through the chest and twice through the leg.

Major Downie, and Lieutenants Sinclair, Demarest, DeGray, and Boyd were severely wounded.

Lieutenant Maginnis noted that only five out of 21 line officers were fit for next day's duty. He turned his H Company over to another. Maginnis had gone in with 35 men. Thirteen were killed; 17 were wounded; five remained for duty.

Maginnis also reported that the Regiment's casualties occurred on a patch of sward about 100 yards square—with the enemy leaving his dead, wounded, and many prisoners.

Night came, and with it the sad and gruesome task of removing the wounded, and burying the dead. It has been recorded that the survivors of that day's battle went out after dark searching for their battle-mates and buddies. It is not hard to visualize the tired men of both sides, moving among the dead and wounded, their candles and lanterns shedding irregular light on the dark forms dotting the forward slope of Cemetery Ridge. One such was Patrick Taylor, looking for Isaac Lyman dead of shrapnel wounds. The young diarist was found, and buried that night, and his diary finished by his brother.

Night, and an end to fighting, but not an end to battle. Those who were left of the First Minnesota shed no tears about what had happened. They merely returned to their bivouac of the previous night, falling asleep on their arms, there to await another day's battle. They were later joined by Companies C, F, and L, the Sharpshooters, who had been detached to support Battery I, First U S Artillery.

The lightning had missed the Minnesota men at Fredericksburg, and again at Chancellorsville. It hit them hard on the Second Day and would call on the remainder on the Third Day.

Having lost, in less than an hour's fighting, 82% of the Regiment's roster, there was no quit in the hearts and minds of the 47 Minnesotans who reported themselves 'equipped and available' for duty.

On the morning of the 3rd Day, the Minnesotans, having their morning coffee and bacon, had no notion, nor did anyone in II Corps have a notion what lightning would strike them, and who it would strike. Lee had called in his corps commanders, and it fell to Longstreet to direct an attack at the Union center, using the only fresh uncommitted troops available: George Pickett's Virginians, 15,000 of the best. Longstreet was reluctant and tried to tease an alternate attack out of Lee, but it did no good. Having failed twice, Lee was in no mood, and Longstreet reluctantly gave Pickett the nod. He was to attack after an artillery bombardment that would suppress Federal artillery and the II Corps infantry. That was the thinking and that was the plan.

The lightning chose the II Corps on Cemetery ridge one mile distant. Victory for Lee would be a complete breakthrough at angle in the stone fence at a small 'clump of trees'.

What Lee and what Pickett did not know was that at that 'clump of trees' the First Minnesota was waiting for the storm to begin. When it did, the Minnesotans showed their contempt by falling into a deep sleep.

The First Minnesota attacked down this slope into the woods through which Plum Run snakes. View is west-from the First Minnesota monument, Distance to the fence line is 250 paces. Beyond the fence, at Plum Run, the Minnesota bayonet attack halted the advance of Alabama and Florida regiments.

A section of the Union line south of The Angle, with the First Minnesota monument at the center of the photograph. The Angle itself is marked by the solitary tree on the horizon, immediately to the right of the Minnesota obelisk. The Copse of Trees, towards which Pickett's troops charged is shown at the right edge of this figure. Sixty-two Minnesota infantrymen formed a line parallel to the monument, facing west, but attacked toward the Angle when the fence was breached, and helped seal off the penetration. Stones, bayonets, clubbed rifles and fists were used to repel the rebel advance.

Chapter Eleven

The Third Day

FOR THE MINNESOTA troopers, the Third Day came clear and bright.Roll call was answered by sixty two men and officers present and ready for duty, just about six men per company. There was some firing at Culp's Hill in the north, with the rebels being driven. There was firing at the Round Tops in the south.

Not long after sunrise, the regiment, commanded by Captain Nathan Messick, moved into the brigade line. The Minnesotans passed the full regiments of Stannard's Vermont Brigade, with their new uniforms and shining brass, then forming up on division left. The whole of the Minnesota First could not muster enough men to fill a company of the least of that brigade's regiments, yet....

Yet they were ready for duty, and it made no difference whether they had a thousand men or sixty two, They were still the Minnesota First—and they would fight.

Messick led his men to a position slightly to the left of the Angle in the stonewall described previously by General Gibbon. The troops busied themselves making a slight barricade of stones, fence rails, and knapsacks filled with dirt. The barricade was a little over knee high. The men lay down behind it, many of them fell fast asleep.

For the Third Day, Lee planned to attack the Union center with a frontal assault by 15,000 men; preceded by an artillery barrage by every available gun. He felt confident of success, although Longstreet told Lee that no 15,000 men ever born could take the ridge. Lee felt confident: he had Major General George Edward Pickett, 38, in charge of a fresh division, 15 regiments strong, all Virginians willing to give it a try—against their better judgement.

Minnesota meets Virginia

At about 1pm, the Confederate artillery line on Seminary Ridge fired a volley that split Sunday in half.. The Union began a strong counter-battery fire, which was discontinued to cool the guns, and to trick the confederates into believing that they were knocking out Union artillery piece by piece.

The firing woke up the sleepers in the Minnesota Regiment. Many, seeing the stuff go harmlessly overhead, went back to sleep. When the bombardment stopped, the tension reached its height. All eyes strained westward, toward Pickett's line of battle a mile away. Pickett's infantry slowly issued from their woodland cover, formed two lines, with some overlapping to three, strongly supported in the flanks.

It has been told in hundreds of accounts how straight the Confederate alignment was, how slowly they began marching toward the Union line, with blood red battle flags held high above their gray masses, bayonets agleam in the sunlight; how the Union artillery, seemingly destroyed, cut gaps in the rebel lines; how the rebels closed the gaps; continued up the slope, apparently unconcerned and arrogant in their suffering; and focused on that "clump of trees" behind the Angle in the stone wall fronting Gibbon's division.

Working the Angle

Lochren described the approach of the rebel line:

"*When about 60 rods distant from our line our division opened with musketry, and the slaughter was very great; but instead of hesitating, the step was changed to double-quick, and they rushed to the charge. But whether because Hancock here wheeled Stannard's Vermont Brigade to enfilade their right flank in passing, or for some other cause, their front opened at this time, and perhaps one-*

quarter of their force on Pickett's right here deflected further to their right, and were met and disposed of by the gallant Vermonters. The remainder of the charging force at the same time diverged or changed direction to its left, and passing from our front diagonally under our fire, and that of Hall's Brigade on our right, charged the position held by Webb's Second Brigade of our division, forcing back the 69th and 71st Pennsylvania Regiments, and capturing Cushing's Battery which had swept them with canister.

But as soon as Pickett's force had passed our front, our brigade (Harrow's) ran to the right for the threatened point, passing in rear of Hall's Brigade, which, as soon as uncovered, wheeled to the right to strike the enemy's flank. So that, by the time the Confederates had captured Cushing's Battery, our brigade, mingled with Webb's, was in front of it, in a strong, though confused line at a few rods distance. Just here we were joined by Captain Farrell with Company C, released from provost guard to resist this attack. The fire from both sides, so near to each other, was deadly while it lasted. Corporal Dehn, the last of our color guard then carrying our tattered flag, was here shot through the hand and the flag staff cut in two.

"Henry D. O'Brien of Company E instantly seized the flag by the remnant of the staff. Whether the command to charge was given by any general officer I do not know. My impression then was that it came as a spontaneous outburst from the men, and instantly the line precipitated itself upon the enemy. O'Brien, who then had the broken staff and tatters of our battle flag, with his characteristic bravery and impetuosity sprang with it to the front at the first sound of the word charge, and rushed right up to the enemy's line keeping it noticeably in advance of every other color. My feeling at that instant blamed his rashness in so risking its capture. But the effect was electrical. Every man of the First Minnesota sprang forward to protect its flag, and the rest rushed with them upon the enemy.

Between the rocks and the hard faces

"The bayonet was used here for a few minutes, and cobblestones, with which the ground was well covered, filled the air, being thrown by those in the rear, over the heads of their comrades. The struggle was desperate and deadly while it lasted, but was soon over. Most of the Confederates remaining threw down their arms and surrendered, a very few escaping. Marshall Sherman of Company C here captured the colors of the 28th Virginia Regiment. Our men were at once most kind and attentive to the three or four thousand prisoners, giving them refreshments from canteens and haversacks."

O'Brien was wounded several times, and was awarded the Congressional Medal of Honor for leading the First Minnesota in to action on the Third Day. Corporal W N Irvine (D Company) grabbed the flag from him. Messick and Farrell were killed; command passed to Captain Coates, who appointed Lochren adjutant.

Sergeant John Plummer described the fighting this way, saying each man *"acted as though he felt what was at stake in the contest, and did all in their power to drive the enemy, without regard to officers, or whether there was any or not.*

"Our boys felt bully during the fight, and no one thought of running, or of the danger. We took revenge for what they had done to our poor fellows the day before, and never had had such a chance before. Most of us fired over twenty [rounds], and at close range enough to do splendid execution; and if we didn't kill some secesh in that battle, we never did, and I fear never will during the war.'

Sergeant Alfred Carpenter wrote later: *"For two hours we had fought desperately. Our muskets became so heated we could no longer handle them. We dropped them and picked up those of the wounded. Our cartridges gave out. We rifled the boxes of the dead. Artillerymen from the disabled pieces in our rear sprang forward, and seizing guns and cartridges from the wounded, fought by our side as infantrymen. Many of the men became deaf, and did not recover their hearing for a day or two. It was a grand and terrible scene.*

Private Marshall Sherman, C Company, was later awarded the Congressional Medal of Honor for capturing the 28th Virginia's regimental colors during the melee.

After the battle, George Knight wrote a friend: *Well, we mowed them down—twas Fredericksburg reversed—*

the first line went down in no time and the others broke—many throwing down their arms and rushing for our lines—Perhaps we didn't feel good when we saw them scatter? It appears their officers had told them that the Militia was fighting them, and would break and run at their approach—but they found it somewhat different. As one of their man gave himself up he says—'Militia be damned—we've seen these flags before'"

Sergeant James Wright remembered how quickly it ended:

"As soon as the smoke lifted sufficiently to permit us to see, all that could be seen of the mighty force was scattered and running to the rear. That is—all that were able to run. The bodies of many unfortunate victims marked the course of the assault. Some of these lay still, where they had fallen, and others were trying to find some safer place. It is very encouraging, at a time like that, when you have done your best, and know it, to see the backs of your enemies, and the space between you and them widening. It was so satisfactory that our fellows could not refrain from cheering as we ceased firing, and realized the situation. It was an occasion worthy of cheers—if ever—despite the fact that many were dead and dying."

But some Union soldiers were slow to realize what had just happened. According to Lieutenant Harmon: *"When the rebs were throwing down their arms and surrendering by the thousands, General Hays rode along the line swearing like a pirate, as the best of men sometimes will in battle. He was trailing a Confederate flag in the dust behind his horse, and was shouting 'Stop firing, you damned fools; don't you know enough to stop firing?. It's all over:! Stop! Stop! Stop!' Then our company was ordered to the front to pick up the straggling prisoners. We advanced clear to the Emmitsburg Road, gathering up the defeated men, and sending them to the rear. I remember that one Confederate private tried to get me to overlook a slightly wounded officer. A little later, a straggler lying in a fence corner drew a bead on me, and was about to shoot, when I covered him with my revolver and told him to drop his gun. He did, too, and it was all I could do to keep the boys from killing him."*

After the rebels retreated and the fighting stopped, many of the troops were on the verge of collapse. As Sergeant Wright recounted later: *"For about 65 hours, we had been under almost constant physical or mental strain,—or both—and had pretty nearly reached the limit of both, and, as soon as the need for further exercise of muscles or will ceased to be imperative, most of the men realized that they were bordering upon a condition of collapse. Those who have not had the experience cannot easily understand how the intense energies necessary to carry men through days of action and excitement, and worked to the utmost in such struggle, use up the vital forces; but those who have 'been there' do not need to be shown."*

Losses for the Regiment were about 44 killed and wounded.

Only 17 were left.

What was left of the battle flag was spliced to a Confederate staff, and carried proudly to the end of the Regiment's tour of duty.

Afterwards, Corporal Carpenter wrote his family on 30 July: *"The field is ours. Can we not go and care for the wounded? No, another attack is expected, and every man must be in his place. Hospital attendants must take care of the wounded till darkness closes down about us. Then we go supperless to sleep; our bed, Mother Earth; our covering, the broad canopy of the starry decked Heavens; the unburied dead sleeping around us."*

The men began to seek out their wounded and dead as dusk approached. Sergeant Wright described it this way: *"We now began to realize that we were getting hungry, and in the gathering darkness we built little fires and made coffee. None of us knew where we were likely to be, or what the morrow would bring for us to do, and, as we drank our coffee, we decided to bury Hamlin that night. Search was made for a spade, and after some time, a shovel was found. With this, a shallow trench was dug beside a walnut tree, near which he had been killed, struck by four bullets. His blanket and tent-cloth were spread in it, he was then laid upon them and covered with the remaining portions. Then those present knelt in silence about him, with uncovered, bowed heads. I do not recall that a word was spoken; but it was a sincere and reverential service fitting the time and the situation. Then we covered him over with the dirt and stones we had thrown out of the trench, and placed at his head a board, oon which his name, company, and regiment, had been marked.'*

Perhaps it is fitting that we close this chapter with another passage from Sergeant Wright, as it sums up the battle and the men from Minnesota.

"It is true we were no longer the sensitive, sentimental youngsters we were when we left our northern homes. Mere sentiment had been knocked out of us by the actual experiences of years of active war; military training, and everyday surroundings had tended to repress expressions of feeling, and had changed us to seasoned soldiers; but no one, though but moderately endowed with common sense, and no more than the ordinary amount of compassion in his makeup, could fail to sympathize, deeply, with the overwhelming amount of suffering that existed, and which they were powerless to relieve. Tens of thousands were suffering from wounds, many were dying every hour; and many still living considered those already dead more fortunate than themselves. It was indeed a blessing, a gracious blessing, that our exhausted bodies, and over-wrought minds could find respite and renewal in sleep.

Chapter Twelve

What It Really Meant

SO ENDED THE Battle of Gettysburg, a Union victory which cost the winners 3,155 killed, 14,529 wounded, and 5,365 captured or missing.

Gettysburg marked the real beginning of the Army of the Potomac as an army, with leadership the troops could depend on, to lead it to final victory over Lee. That would come twenty months later, at Appomattox.

For the Confederates, the high cost of losing: 2,592 killed, 12,709 wounded, and 5,150 captured or missing. The defeat at Gettysburg, and the loss of Vicksburg the same day, marked the beginning of the end for the Confederacy. From then on, the Confederacy declined, losing the power to wage any offensive that might bring it victory, although it would score occasional isolated victories which had no real meaning—but to the casualties.

For General Lee and his Army of Northern Virginia, it meant the end of an era, and the onset of decay and failure. His army would exercise proficiency in defensive warfare—digging trenches and erecting fieldworks, and waiting for the Federals to assault them. There came a time, though, when the digging had to end, a time when the infantry had to come out in to the open, a time when, finally, all of their bravery and finesse could not save them, a time to end counter-productive fighting and surrender and go home.

For the 175 men of the First Minnesota, who mustered on 30 July, there were still nine months of service before them. It was, despite its less than two company size, a winning regiment, more proficient and deadly in the work of arms than some full-strength regiments in the Army.

After the battle of Gettysburg, many of the men wondered if there would be enough men left to muster out come the Spring of '64. Nobody seemed to care. None of the Division or Corps Commanders seemed to think that their service or casualties called for special privileges, or non-combatant duty in the rear. General Meade did not think so, and best of all, none of the men of the Regiment seemed to think so either.

They were that kind of men in that kind of army.

Post Script to the gentle reader

In writing this short account of the action of the First Minnesota Regiment of Volunteers, the writers used the words of the soldiers who were in the battle; no attempt has been made to analyze the contradictions in the various statements by these participants because the purpose of this small work was simply to tell the story of some very brave men as briefly as we could because we could not reconcile these contradictions, especially those that relate to casualties. We felt that we would simply state the different numbers and present you with the casualty lists drawn from the company rosters derived from those given in Minnesota in the Civil and Indian Wars (1890) and the company rosters in the History of the First Regiment Minnesota Volunteer Infantry by Return Holcomb (1915). Our casualty lists made reference to the 42 KIAs and 37 later died of wounds (DOW) = 79 men, as listed in John Busey's These Honored Dead (1986) and highlighted their names in the text. These casualties are mainly for 2 July.

What is even worse, our study shows that each account of casualties varies. Captain Coates said that there were 232 casualties, which included six missing. In the report of 31 August, the total is 245, none missing.

Total casualties were originally reported as 82% of the 262 men in the eight companies engaged, but Busey in his study uses the losses reported in the Official Records and that record says 330 men with 50 KIA 173 WIA, and one missing = 67.9% (for both days).

If we argue, from pride, we should believe the 82% figure, but if we argue from humanitarian principles we should believe the 67.9% figure, as that means the same mission was accomplished with fewer losses.

We are going to write a companion piece to this which will try to resolve this question of casualties in a book on the Minnesota First called the *Thunderbolt in Blue* which will also go into finer detail about all of the battles and actions of this regiment.

The main drawback to completion of any book, is the high cost of research, in both time and dollars. And if writers earn their livelihood from writing, the cost of research can be greater than any return from royalties, if not enough books are sold, and that is the second drawback: being brave enough to do the work without really knowing how successful, a particular book will be.

We believe that The First Minnesota at Gettysburg will justify our bravery in publishing it, and we thank you for taking your eyes this far.

We welcome any comments on how to improve this work, and invite you to send us any information you may have, or copies of photographs, newspaper clippings, etc, that we might apply to these works. As an example, we heard from Mr Steve Bartel, a descendant of Alozo Hayden, Company D, who was killed on 2 July, at Gettysburg. Mr Bartel was kind enough to send us a genealogy of the Hayden family that goes back several hundred years to England. It is information like this that adds depth to the human dimension of our story, dimensions that mean more than statistics.

Appendices A & B

First Minnesota Casualty Lists

Notes on casualties:

Casualty lists, by company, for 2 and 3 July are in Appendix A and B, respectivcly.

1. The number of officers and men reported to the State Adjutant on 31 May 1863 was: 24 officers and 318 men = 342, all ranks.

2. On 30 June at Uniontown, Maryland, a regimental payday listed 27 officers and 358 enlisted men = 385 soldiers, all ranks. Company L was a detachment of Berdan's 1st Regiment of Sharpshooters under Captain Berger who commanded three officers and 28 men to make the total complement = 416 officers and men available for duty at Gettysburg.

3. Eight companies (A, B, D, E, G, H, I, K) charged on the second day. Captain Maginnis said that 215 officers and men were in the charge. C,F and L companies had special assignments and did not charge.

4. The casualty lists are derived from the list shown on pages 375 and 376 of Minnesota in the Civil and Indian Wars, Pioneer Press, St Paul, Minnesota 1890. These lists show the killed and wounded by company for all enlisted men at Gettysburg and generally show the date on which a particular casualty occurred. The list for officers is taken from the company and staff rosters of the same book, and shown separately on page B-12.

5. Boldfaced entries are casualties verified by John W Busey (These Honored Dead, Longstreet House, 1988) from various sources, listing 42 KIA; 37 DOW = 79 total both days.

6. There is some controversy on the numbers involved: exactly how many men were in the eight companies that made the charge is disputed and some uncertainty about the exact number killed and wounded, even among those who were there, and among those who researched the casualty records. What we know is that the First went into Gettysburg with 11 companies = 416 soldiers, all ranks. Of the 265 men who Captain Maginnis said were present for duty on the second day, and about 62 men (all companies) available for duty on the third day. In the action at the Angle, 44 men were reported killed and wounded. This meant that there were 18 men on their feet to celebrate the 4th of July.

7. The Regiment did recover slightly: The muster of 30 July showed 175 men, all ranks, available for duty. On its way home to Minnesota, the Regiment attended a banquet in Washington (February 1864) It is assumed that the 309 members who attended that banquet were mustered out inMay of that year when the death certificate of the First Minnesota Volunteer Regiment was signed at Fort Snelling. Some of the men joined the 1st Battalion Minnesota Volunteers and carried the spirit of the First Regiment to the end of the war.

8. Our word war comes from the German word *werra*, which means confusion, and that is exactly what war is: confusion. No where is it more evident than in the statistics of battle.

Battle: Gettysburg	*Date: 2 July 1863*	*Company A*
KIA Name & Rank	*WIA* Name & Rank	*DOW* Name & Rank
1. Elder, Julius (C)	1. Adams, Lucius (P)	1. Brandt, Clark (P), leg amputated at knee, died 7/21
2. Hauser, John (P)	2. Farquhar, Daniel (P)	2. Crawley, Frederick T (C), died 7/20
3. Keyes, James (C)	3. Giser, Frederick (P)	3. Glave, Frederick (P), leg amputated, died 8/03
4. Kratka, Charles A (P)	4. Hausdorf, Charles F (S)	4. Marks, Peter (C), leg amputated, died 7/24
5. Loomis, Charles C (P) (Transferred US Cav 10/62, but listed as KIA here.)	5. Lyons, Steven (C)	5. Nickel, Henry (P), right thigh fractured, died 8/10
6. Miller, William F (P)	6. Mowry, Rascellas (P)	6. Simonson, Hans M (P), thigh fractured, gunshot, died 8/3
7. Schmucker, James (C)	7. Muller, Charles (P)	7. Wright, Henry C (S), died 7/5
8. Wagner, Warren (P)	8. Sanders, Benjamin (P)	
9. Wilson, John (P)	9. Steen, Charles (1st Sgt), leg amputated	
	10. Thiem, Joseph (P)	

Casualty summary

KIA	***9***
WIA	***10***
DOW	***7***
Total	***26***

Abbreviations used in these lists

P = Private
C = Corporal
S= Sergeant = Sgt
1Sgt = 1st Sergeant
SM = Sergeant-Major
QM = Quarter Master
1Lt = 1st Lieutenant
2Lt = 2nd Lieutenant
Cpt = Captain
Maj = Major
LTC = Lieutenant Colonel
Col = Colonel

KIA=Killed in action
WIA=Wnded in action
DOW=Died of wounds
MIA= Missing in action

Battle: Gettysburg	*Date: 2 July 1863*	*Company B*
KIA **Name & Rank**	***WIA*** **Name & Rank**	***DOW*** **Name & Rank**
10. Bates, William F (P) 11. Koenig, August (P) 12. Nickerson, Samual (S)	11. Arnold, George (P) 12. Aucker, William (P) 13. Carriegiet, Barth (P) 14. Caplazi, Albert (P) 15. Crome, Frederick (Sgt) 16. Densmore, John (Sgt) 17. Erhardt, Moritz (P) 18. Everson, Peter (P) 19. Hamman, Charles (P) 20. Henry, Martin (P) 21. Johnson, David (P) 22. Lord, David (1st Sgt) 23. Marty, Adam (P) 24. Marty, Fridolin (P) 25. Nystedt, Eric (P) 26. Oliver, George (Sgt) 27. Schoenbeck, John (P) 28. Sebers, Albert (P) 29. Stephens, John (C) 30. Wells, Edwin (C)	8. Quist, Andrew P (P) 9. Thompson, Ole (P), left arm amputated, died 8/8 10. Gove, Charles (P), died 7/30 Note: Andrew Quist, above, listed WIA in AGO records. See next column. But not shown mustered out; so presumed dead **Casualty summary** ***KIA 3*** ***WIA 20*** ***DOW 3*** ***Total 26***

Battle: Gettysburg	*Date: 2 July 1863*	*Company C*
KIA Name & Rank	*WIA* Name & Rank	*DOW* Name & Rank
13.Howard, Henry (1st S) 14. Lufkin, Wade (S)		11. Elsworth, John (P), fractured leg amputated, died 7/20 12. Greenwald, Aaron (QM Sgt), died 7/7 13. Howard, Henry (1st Sgt), died 7/3 14. Lufkin, Wade (S), died 7/3

Casualty summary

KIA ***0***
WIA ***0***
DOW ***4***
Total ***4***

Battle: Gettysburg	*Date: 2 July 1863*	*Company D*
KIA	***WIA***	***DOW***
Name & Rank	**Name & Rank**	**Name & Rank**
15. Baker, Charles (P) 16. Hayden, Alonzo (P) 17. Past, Marcus (P) 18. Prime, James (P)	31. Bartlett, George W (P) 32. Bryant, James (C) 33. Geer, Charles (P) 34. Howe, Archibald (P) 35. Kouts, Jacob (C) 36. Nason, Thomas B (C) 37. Noel, Benjamin (P) 38. Perkins, Ellet (Color Sgt) 39. Rines, Charles (P) 40. Robinson, Calvin (Sgt) 41. Smith, William C (P) 42. Smithyman, Joseph (P) 43. Sullivan, Daniel (P) 44. Walsh, James W (P)	15. Allen, Wm (P), shot in thigh, died 7/8 16. Grandy, George (P) died 7/4 17. Lawrence, Irv (P), head wound, died 7/5 18. Mason, Charles, (1Lt), died 8/18 19. Rollins, Franklin (P) died 8/3

Casualty summary

KIA 4
WIA 14
DOW 4
Total 22

Battle: Gettysburg	*Date: 2 July 1863*	*Company E*
KIA **Name & Rank**	***WIA*** **Name & Rank**	***DOW*** **Name & Rank**
19. Davis, John (P) 20. Fowler, Norman (P) 21. Jackins, Isaac (P) 22. Taylor, Isaac (P) 23. Trevor, Joseph (1st Sgt) ***Casualty summary*** ***KIA 5*** ***WIA 18*** ***DOW 3*** ***Total 26***	45. Adams George A (P) 46. Berry, Amos O (P) 47. Berry, Charles A (P) 48. Bradley, Henry C (C) 49. Currie, John (P) 50. Drake, Hiram (P) 51. Fisher, Henry (P) 52. Hill, Jonas R (P) 53. Holden, Wm W (P3) 54. Jefferson, Ernest (P) 55. Losee, Wm H (P) 56. Middlestadt, Vincent (P) 57. Staples, Benjamin (C) 58. Stites, Adam (P) 59. Stites, Samuel (Sgt) 60. Taylor, Mathew F (C) 61. Wait, Daniel H (P) 62. Weaver, Elijah (P)	20. Demerest, David (Lt), died 7/30 21. Mc Kenzie, John (C), right femur, died 8/7 21. Welin, Peter (P), shot in the thigh: amputated, died 7/29

Battle: Gettysburg	*Date: 2 July 1863*	*Company F*
KIA **Name & Rank**	***WIA*** **Name & Rank**	***DOW*** **Name & Rank**
None	63. Abbott, Marion (C) 64. Bachelor, James F (P) 65. King, Levi (P)	22. Squire, Leonard (C), shot in hip, died 7/7

Casualty summary

KIA	***0***
WIA	***3***
DOW	***1***
Total	***4***

Battle: Gettysburg	*Date: 2 July 1863*	*Company G*
KIA	***WIA***	***DOW***
Name & Rank	**Name & Rank**	**Name & Rank**
24. Sawyer, George P (C)	66. Araman, Adam (P)	23. Ernst, Anthony W (P), died 8/5
25. Sisler, Joseph (P)	67. Barton, Dana S (P)	24. Dunham, Phineas (C), thigh fracture, died 7/17
26. Strothman, John (C)	68. Bondurant, Cyrus S (P)	25. Ernst, Anthony W (P), died 8/22
	69. Brown, William W (P)	26. Farnsworth, Jerome (P), died 7/5, (other reference cites 7/23)
	70. Carney, James H (P)	27. Mc Kinstry, John (P), died 8/22
	71. Coen, William G (P)	
	72. Gatzke, John (P)	
	73. Goodrich, Jona (P)	
	74. Hopkins, George (P)	
	75. Lilly, Samuel (P)	
	76. Magee, George (P)	
	77. Mosher, Ludwell (P)	
	78. Reed, Walter S (P)	
	79. Rhorher, John M (P)	

Casualty summary

KIA ***3***
WIA ***14***
DOW ***5***
Total ***22***

Battle: Gettysburg	Date: 2 July 1863	Company H
KIA **Name & Rank**	**WIA** **Name & Rank**	**DOW** **Name & Rank**
27. Ackers, James H (1st Sgt) 28. Clauser, John (P) 29. Drondt, Kellian (P) 30. Essencey, John (C) 31. Hess, Rheinhold (P) 32. Wikoff, William H (Sgt)	None	28. Diehr, Frederick (Sgt), shot in the side, died 7/21: buried in Minnesota plot B-4, Gettysburg **Casualty summary** *KIA* 6 *WIA* 0 *DOW* 1 *Total* 7

Battle: Gettysburg	*Date: 2 July 1863*	*Company I*
KIA **Name & Rank**	***WIA*** **Name & Rank**	***DOW*** **Name & Rank**
33. Ellis, Philander (P) 34. Farrar, Waldo (2LT) 35. Frey, Jos (P) 36. Welch, Byron (P) 37. Woodard, Oscar (Sgt) **Casualty summary** ***KIA 5*** ***WIA 13*** ***DOW 6*** ***Total 24***	80. Abbott, Henry (P) 81. Donavan, Jeremiah (P) 82. Howell, William D (P) 83. Hutchins, Daniel (P) 84. Jackson, Benjamin (P) 85. Knight, Oliver (1st Sgt) * 86. Lawson, Herman (C) 87. Miller, Ernst L (C) 88. Milliken, George A (C) 89. Rabaca, Herman (P) 90. Roe, William J (Sgt) 91. Weaver, Daniel S (P) 92. Wedges, Henry (P) * Knight wounded about noon by artillery fire; not in charge.	29. Freeze, Jacob (P), died 8/2 30. Hale, Edward P (P), leg amputated, died 9/12 31. Paul, Edwin (P), leg fractured & amputated, died 7/13 32. Peck, William N (C). died 7/4 33. Roe, William (Sgt). died7/2 34. Wellman, William F (C), leg amputated at thigh, died 8/2

Battle: Gettysburg	*Date: 2 July 1863*	*Company K*
KIA **Name & Rank**	***WIA*** **Name & Rank**	***DOW*** **Name & Rank**
38. Geisreiter, Jacob (P) 39. Gore, Leslie P (P) 40. Smith, Augustus (P) 41. Taylor, David (P) 42. Vosz, Peter (P) 43. Winters, Henry C (P) 44. Wright, Randolph (C)	93. Behr, Charles (P) 94. Carpenter, Alfred (Sgt) 95. Durfee, Chester (P) 96. Eaton, Joseph (P) 97. Einfeldt, John (C) 98. Ely, Charles (P) 99. Goddard, Charles (P) 100. Hanson, Lewis (P) 101. Keiley, Timothy (C) 102. Kinyon, William H (P) 103. Marvin, Mathew (Sgt) 104. North, Charles (C) 105. Tenney, Samuel (P) 106. Towner, James (P)	35. Durr, Israel (P), shot in the side, died 7/6) **Casualty summary** ***KIA 7*** ***WIA 14*** ***DOW 1*** ***Total 22***

Battle: Gettysburg	Date: 2 July 1863	Company L
KIA Name & Rank	**WIA** Name & Rank	**DOW** Name & Rank
None Note: Attached to the Minnesota 1st, this detachment of Berdan's 1st US Sharpshooters was deployed as artillery support on 2 July. It joined the Regiment on 3 July, at the Angle. Their strength on 30 June was three officers and 38 men = 41 total	None	None

Casualty summary

KIA 0
WIA 0
DOW 0
Total 0

Battle: Gettysburg	Date: 3 July 1863	Company A
KIA Name & Rank	**WIA** Name & Rank	**DOW** Name & Rank
None	107. Dehn, John W (C) 108. Devlin, Michael (P) 109. Dooley, William A H (Sgt) 110. Drake, Charles (P) 111. Simonson, Hans (P)	None

Casualty summary

KIA 0
WIA 5
DOW 0
Total 5

Battle: Gettysburg	Date: 3 July 1863	Company B
KIA Name & Rank	WIA Name & Rank	DOW Name & Rank
None	112. Blanchard, Rufus G (P) 113. Tanner, Joseph A (P)	None

Casualty summary

KIA: ***0***
WIA ***2***
DOW ***0***
Total ***2***

Battle: Gettysburg	*Date: 3 July 1863*	*Company C*
KIA Name & Rank	***WIA*** Name & Rank	***DOW*** Name & Rank
45. Ellsworth, John (P)	114. Atherton, Miner (P)	None
46. Greenwald, Aaron (C)	115. Clancy, Daniel (P)	
47. Howard, Henry H (1st Sgt)	116. Gilman, James (P)	
48. Lufkin, Wade (Sgt)	117. Hayford, Faxon (P)	
	118. Kreuger, Andrew J (Sgt)	
	119. Leonard, Maurice F (P)	
	120. Squires, Gideon (C)	

Casualty summary

KIA ***4***
WIA ***7***
DOW ***0***
Total ***11***

Battle: Gettysburg	Date: 3 July 1863	Company D
KIA Name & Rank	**WIA** Name & Rank	**DOW** Name & Rank
49. Grandy, George (P)	None	None

Casualty summary

KIA	1
WIA	0
DOW	0
Total	1

Battle: Gettysburg	*Date: 3 July 1863*	*Company E*
KIA **Name & Rank**	***WIA*** **Name & Rank**	***DOW*** **Name & Rank**
None	121. O'Brien, Henry D (C) NOTE: Color bearer on 3 July; wounded at the Angle.	None

Casualty summary

KIA	***0***
WIA	***1***
DOW	***0***
TOT	***1***

Battle: Gettysburg	*Date: 3 July 1863*	*Company F*
KIA Name & Rank	***WIA*** Name & Rank	***DOW*** Name & Rank
50. Hamlin, Philip R (Sgt) 51. Squire, Leonard (C)	122. Barber, Horatio N (P) 123. Burgetorf, Henry (P) 124. Decker, Artemus L (P) 125. Hubles, Charles E (P) 126. Jacobs, Romulus (P)	None

Casualty summary

KIA	***2***
WIA	***5***
DOW	***0***
Total	***7***

Battle: Gettysburg	*Date: 3 July 1863*	*Company G*
KIA **Name & Rank**	*WIA* **Name & Rank**	*DOW* **Name & Rank**
None	127. Ernst, Anthony (P) 128. Jones, Anthony (C)	None

Casualty summary

KIA: 00
WIA: 02
DOW: 00
TOT: 02

Battle: Gettysburg	*Date: 3 July 1863*	*Company H*
KIA **Name & Rank**	***WIA*** **Name & Rank**	***DOW*** **Name & Rank**
None	129. Bradbury, George W (P) 130. Cronkhite, Samuel S (P) 131. Dockin, John (P) 132. Graham, Thomas (P) 133. Smith, Benjamin (P)	None

Casualty summary

KIA	***0***
WIA	***5***
DOW	***0***
Total	***5***

Battle: Gettysburg	*Date: 3 July 1863*	*Company I*
KIA Name & Rank	***WIA*** Name & Rank	***DOW*** Name & Rank
None	134. Lawson, Herman (C) 135. Richards, William R (Sgt) 136. Roe, William (Sgt)	None

Casualty summary

KIA	***0***
WIA	***3***
DOW	***0***
Total	***3***

Battle: Gettysburg	Date: 3 July 1863	Company K
KIA Name & Rank	**WIA** Name & Rank	**DOW** Name & Rank
52. Vasz, Peter (P) 53. Wright, Randolph (P)	137. Durfee, Chester H (P)	None

Casualty summary

KIA	2
WIA	1
DOW	0
Total	3

Battle: Gettysburg	Date: 3 July 1863	Company L
KIA Name & Rank	**WIA** Name & Rank	**DOW** Name & Rank
54. Brown, Sylvester (P)	138. Baker, Ozias P (P) 139. Coleman, William C (P)	None

Casualty summary

KIA	1
WIA	2
DOW	0
Total	3

In addition to the casulties listed in these appendix tables, the following company and staff officers were injured or killed at Gettysburg.

1. Colonel William Colvill, wounded
2. Lt Colonel Charles Powell Adams, wounded
3. Major Mark Downie. Formerly, captain of Company B, wounded.
4. Adjutant John Peller, wounded
5. Captain Thomas Sinclair, Company E, wounded
6. Captain Louis Muller, (formerly Company B), killed
7. 1st Lt William May, Company B, wounded
8. Captain Wilson Farrell, Company C, killed
9. 1st Lt William Harmon, Company C, wounded
10. 2nd Lt Charles Mason, Company C (formerly D), died of wounds on 18 Aug 1863
11. Captain Christian Heffelfinger, Company D, wounded
12. 1st Lt Ellet Perhins, Company D, wounded
13. 2nd Lt William Harmon, Company D, wounded
14. 1st Lt David Demerest, Company E, died of wounds on 29 July 1863
15. Captain Nathan Messick, Company G, killed
16. 1st Lt James DeGray, Company G, wounded
17. Captain Charles Adams, Company H, wounded
18. 2nd Lt Waldo Farrar, Company I, killed
19. Captain Joseph Periam, Company K, died of wounds, 7 July 1863

A two-photo sequence of the loading and firing of a '12-pounder' cannon, a standard artillery piece at Gettysburg. The eight-man crew is reloading the cannon, and the smoke from a previous blank-round still lingers in the air about them. The piece is shown in the unlimbered position. The limber is the two-wheeled unit to the left. It contains ammuniton and accessories necessary to the operation of the gun. Rate of fire: 2-4 rounds/minute depending on the skill of the gunners.

Re-enactment team firing of a '12-pounder' cannon, at the Gettysburg battlefield.(June 2002).It is not hard to imagine the cloud of smoke a hundred-fifty cannon could generate when fired in unison for several hours on a hot windless day. Add the smoke of tens of thousands of muskets to this gunsmoke...

Other Books by The Info Devel Press

Frank Luke, the September Rampage

The Red Baron, Manfred von Richthofen

Military Quotations 2000

Military Quotations 2001

Pray Tell, Private Hell (Civil War poems by Steven Bartel)

A Short, but Foamy, History of Beer

67615747R00046

Made in the USA
Lexington, KY
21 September 2017